Marlon Smith

WHAT'S UP?

A Solution Guide for Today's Young People

Illustrated by

Malcolm Aaron

Designed by

Myrna M. Urmanita

FIRST EDITION 1993

What's Up?
A Solution Guide for Today's Young People

Copyright © 1993 by Marlon Smith

ISBN   0-9643564-0-6

Success By Choice
25125 Santa Clara Street
Suite 321
Hayward, CA. 94544
(510) 887-1311

Printed in the United States of America.

ACKNOWLEDGMENTS

Love and support from my family of friends and relatives enabled my ideas to evolve into this God-inspired piece of literature.

A special thanks goes to **Barbara Murphy and Mark Shepherd** who rolled up their sleeves and got "busy" in the final stages as this book crystallized.

And from the beginning, there have been three special individuals who gave relentless hours to complete this book.

My Aunt Thelma was always there for me, taking time from her busy schedule to review and edit each manuscript revision. I thank you for your belief in me.

Malcolm Aaron and his mighty pen enhanced this book with thrilling drawings that will no doubt capture the reader's attention. I thank you for your dedication, Malcolm.

Myrna Urmanita stayed up many long nights in front of her computer, positioning pictures and highlighting main points to keep ALL readers interested from beginning to end. I thank your son, Jonathan, and daughter, Janelle, for being so understanding. And I thank you for your wisdom.

Again, this book is not a one-person project. But rather, it is the culmination of many insights and experiences shared by family and friends. I love you all.

Thank you **mom and dad** for taking the time to instill true morals and values within me. If it were not for your unconditional love and support, I would not be who I am. Thank you for being there for me. And to each of my brothers, Sean, Greg and Lance, I love you for who you are. You continue to be my inspiration. *Remember, we're the Smith Brothers, strong and proud.*

As of yet, there is one special relationship that I have not mentioned that made this entire book possible. And that is my relationship with God. It was God who inspired me with this book idea. It was God who kept me going when I wanted to give up. And it was God who guided me through every step of the way to this final publication. **Thank You God! I give you ALL the honor and glory.**

About the Illustrator

Malcolm Aaron has always known that being an artist was his destiny. Growing up in Upper Marlboro, Maryland, art allowed Malcolm to express himself. Malcolm graduated from Largo Senior High School where he was a two-time winner of the outstanding achievement award in art. Malcolm also served as art editor of the school newspaper and yearbook staff. He was honored with the Lions award given to an outstanding senior. After graduation, Malcolm matriculated at North Carolina Agriculture and Technical State University in Greensboro, North Carolina. Malcolm majored in Art Design and put his talents to good use by once again joining the school newspaper and yearbook staff. He served as art editor for four years and received several awards from the campus newspaper. Malcolm was also the publicity chairman for Alpha Phi Alpha Fraternity and the Panhellenic Council. After graduating from North Carolina A&T, Malcolm returned to Maryland where he became a free-lance artist. His first published artwork was included in the book, "From the Browder File: An Anthology of Essays on Afrocentric Thought," by Anthony Browder. Two other book projects followed. In 1989, Malcolm joined the Midway Agency, a design firm in Chapel Hill, North Carolina. His responsibility included producing camera-ready artwork for logos, tee shirts, editorial cartoons, etc. Malcolm has produced illustrations for the University of North Carolina football team. Sports View magazine and the Town of Chapel Hill head the lists of his clients. Early in 1994, Malcolm left the Midway Agency to form his own company, Mal-Ice Enterprises. Recently, Malcolm was published for the fifth time, painting the cover illustration for Dr. Na'im Akbar's "Light from Ancient Africa." Malcolm hopes to continue his success in the industry by continuing to impact people through his art.

Malcolm lives in Chapel Hill, North Carolina where he continues his mission as an artist.

About the Designer

If you ask Myrna what she designs, you will probably get an answer like, "What do you need?" Everyone who has experienced working with Myrna knows that she will always come up with a solution for your graphic need no matter what it is. Myrna Urmanita received her Art training at The California College of Arts and Crafts in Oakland, California. She received her Bachelor of Fine Arts degree in Graphic Design. After graduation, Myrna experienced the real world of design. She started out as a Forms Designer for a major insurance company in San Francisco. There, she was introduced to the corporate world and learned the fundamentals of survival in the business world, people relations and working with the system............................things you don't learn in school. Through the years, Myrna was an Art Director, an Advertising Director, and a Designer for corporations in both private industry and the public schools. Myrna began free-lancing right after college and soon opened up her own business, Urmanita & Associates. Myrna's versatility in design includes graphics design, special events design, point of purchase display, corporate identity, and anything else a client might come up with. She attributes all her talents and her sensitivity to meeting her client's needs to God. Everyone who has come to work with Myrna experiences her energy and the excitement she brings to their graphic needs. She believes that success for her only comes when she can help someone else succeed. Design is not just a job or a career for Myrna, it is a life-style. It is not unusual to find Myrna working late hours into the evening, designing diligently on her computer to help meet her client's needs —call her at 1:00 in the morning and find her at her computer or even with a client. Myrna is a designer, who cares about her client's image because it is a reflection of her own.

Myrna lives in Fremont, California with her fourteen year old son, Jonathan, and her nine year old daughter, Janelle. They are following their mother's footsteps—both are artistically talented, too.

ABOUT THE AUTHOR

Today, Marlon Christopher Smith is a young man who is on a mission. However, he has not always been blessed with this focus. As a young person, there were times when Marlon did not appreciate his true worth. He lacked confidence in his abilities, and to further complicate matters, he struggled in school. No matter how much time he spent on his studies, some class material was just too "HARD" for him to comprehend. Many questioned his future.

But Marlon turned his life around! His confidence soared and his academic performance reached all new heights, with one report card even displaying all "A's." Nevertheless, some people still doubted his abilities. However, with a new perspective on life, Marlon was not going to let someone's opinion of him become his reality.

Marlon attended the University of Virginia where he studied electrical engineering. With an energized commitment, Marlon beat the odds and graduated with a Bachelor of Science degree in electrical engineering. As a college student, Marlon's proudest moment came when he founded Street Academics, a high school outreach program. Each week, Marlon and his college friends went into various high schools to share success strategies with younger students. Through his involvement, Marlon learned the power of "giving."

Marlon's corporate experience includes working for two Fortune-500 corporations, IBM and Hewlett-Packard. Growing to realize his personal mission, Marlon resigned from his corporate position at Hewlett-Packard on January 15, 1992.

Today, Marlon can be found empowering our global society by helping people realize their true potential through his company, Success By Choice. He has been blessed with an opportunity to inspire, entertain and motivate thousands of individuals. He even had the opportunity to travel throughout South Africa on a 16-day speaking tour where he empowered various communities with his inspiring message of "Embracing Diversity." Marlon continues to utilize his engineering training by developing innovative, multi-media presentations. And because of this, Marlon is recognized as the **"High-Tech" Motivator.**

TABLE OF CONTENTS

TABLE OF CONTENTS

Forward

No matter what has happened in your past, today is a new day! SO GET EXCITED!

Yes, it is true that life does not always turn out the way that we desire. But remember this, "All of us struggle with difficult challenges, obstacles, trials and tribulations. For some, they are empowered by growing through these experiences. While unfortunately, for others, these issues become roadblocks which strangle and choke their dreams."

Two roadblocks, in particular, that many young people continue to deal with are:
1) Suffering from low self-esteem and
2) Failing in school.

"What's Up?" is written with the purpose of helping you maximize your TRUE potential.

> The first chapter, "Choices In The Maze," will enlighten you to the power of your choices.

> The second chapter, "Suffering From Low Self-Esteem And Lacking Self-Confidence," will help you realize your many blessings.

> The third chapter, "Failing In School," will inspire you as you come to understand the importance of an education.

> The fourth chapter, "Failing In College," will empower you with strategies for maximizing your potential both inside and outside the classroom.

> And finally, the last chapter, "Claim Your Success," will offer a thrilling conclusion as well as a personal challenge.

The power of this book lies in the fact that you will be inspired to THINK about your future. By answering various questions and completing the exercises throughout this book, you will realize the power of your choices in determining your future. You will be motivated to THINK first before taking any action because every decision leads to a certain consequence. And at the conclusion, you will claim your success because you will realize that "Your Success Is Your Choice."

Dedicated to you...

This book is dedicated to you —
my young brothers and sisters...

to maximize your true potential,
to empower yourselves,
to learn from your past,
and...

    to become pioneers of your future.

Life is Full of Choices!

"Come on Nolram! No one will ever know."

Stunned, I question myself, "What should I do?"

My friends want me to do it but I know it's wrong.

"Nolram, you're DOWN with us, right? Let's get busy."

I freeze. I can't move. What do I do?

What do I do? Help Me!

Here I am...
with another pressing
issue on my mind.

What should I do?

I just don't know.
I'm so confused.
My life is filled with
so many choices.

And sometimes,
my decisions lead
to more problems.
There have even been
times when I cried while
I tried to figure it all out.

Is this how it is for you? Is your life sometimes like a maze, full of choices and decisions?

Do your decisions always lead to positive consequences?

Everyday, you make decisions. Some are small, while others are big.

Think about it.

Right now, there's a critical decision to be made. What are you going to do with this book? It's in your hands. Which of the following three doors will you choose?

Door #1
Close the book and throw it away.

Door #2
Skim through the book only looking at the pictures.

Door #3
Read each page slowly, taking time to answer all the questions.

Which door do you choose?

Life is Full of Choices!

In life, you're faced with many choices and decisions. For me, life is like a maze with three doors at the entrance. Each day, I feel as if I'm facing those three doors. Every door leads to an unknown path and frankly, I'm a little scared! I don't want to make the wrong choice, but which one do I choose?

Choices are difficult to make. I've had to endure some challenging consequences in the past because I've gone through the wrong door. And there have even been times when I thought I was on the right path, only to come to a dead end.

However, today, I think I'm on the right path. I'm feeling good and life is great! But...

Oh, no! Another set of doors!
Here I go again! Which do I choose?
What do I do? Someone......

By choosing Door #3, you will be empowered.

Consider this book to be a gift behind that door. .... You're not going to throw it away, right?

Life is Full of Choices!

As we all know, life can be confusing at times. I know, I've been there.

I remember my mom constantly hassling me. She would say over and over, "Nolram, this is your life. You either choose to be successful, or by default, you choose to fail. You have a mind, Nolram. USE IT."

My mom was right. This is my life. And if it's to be, then it's up to me. I think life is similar to a maze: a maze composed of many doors, each one leading to life decisions about "education," "sex," "peer pressure," "drugs," "money," etc.

Life is Full of Choices!

Everyday, we make decisions that affect the quality of our lives. Sometimes, we don't recognize the importance of our choices. When I was younger, I sure didn't. I lived without a care. I wasn't concerned about the consequences of my decisions.

I just lived day to day. That's just how it was. However, this all changed one day— the day I was suspended from school for fighting. After that, for some reason I became more aware of my life's direction. I realized that I was NOT on the path which was taking me closer to my dreams.

After the fight, I sat alone in the principal's office and reflected about why I had been suspended. I can replay my mental video of Principal Kohkinus saying, in seeming slow motion,...

"Nolram... You are suspended!"

Life is Full of Choices!

Wow, what a trip, huh? For the first time in my life, I realized that I was responsible for what happened to me. I couldn't blame Principal Kohkinus or my instigating friends, or even my tattletale teacher, Mr. Hemmerson. There were critical CHOICES that I made which led to my suspension. I CHOSE to yell back at Paul, who I believed had disrespected me. When he pushed me, I made the DECISION to confront him rather than walk away. After that, one thing led to another and kids began gathering around, instigating us to fight. And before I knew it, we got into it. Within two minutes, we were being pulled apart by three teachers who had to restrain us. I was then dragged into the principal's office. Before Kohkinus came in to give me yet another lecture, I thought about my future. While I sat there, I came to realize the impact that my choices had made in my life. If I had CHOSEN to act differ- [ently just ten minutes ago, I] would not be sitting in [the principal's office now.] Also, I wouldn't have [to face my mom's anger] when she found out that [I got into trouble. But I] couldn't go back and [redo the past. At the time of] the fight, I believed I [couldn't let Paul get the best] of me. I really didn't [think about any other] choices. All I could think [about was the pain of being] called a *wimp* or a *punk* because I didn't stand my ground. Rather than feel this pain, I felt the temporary pleasure of hearing my friends chant: "Go Nolram, kick his butt!" as I tried to knock Paul's head off. However, I was only focusing on the short-term. I didn't think about the other pain I would feel when my mom found out I was suspended for fighting. As a CONSEQUENCE of my decision to fight, my mother grounded me for a month. I lost all telephone privileges. And that was definitely long-term pain.

> Most of us want pleasure and not pain. And as a result, most of our decisions are based on either gaining pleasure or avoiding pain.

As I sat in Principal Kohkinus's office, I did some serious reflecting about my life and where I was headed. I came to the conclusion that everything I do is for one of two reasons: either to avoid pain or to gain pleasure. Straight up! This maze called "life" is like a roller coaster filled with many pleasurable "ups" and many painful "downs." And for me, I want pleasure and not pain. Because of this, most of my decisions are based on either gaining pleasure or avoiding pain.

You see, the pain of being ridiculed by my friends if I didn't fight, prompted me to fight. I then felt pleasure while hearing my friends chant my name as I fought. However, I wish I had taken some time to think about the consequences before I fought. Once again, I had overlooked the long-term impact of my decision. I felt pain when Principal Kohkinus said "Nolram, you're suspended." And then I experienced even more pain when I encountered my mom's punishment. Just think, if I had only chose to act differently, all of this pain could have been avoided.

Life is Full of Choices!

It really does comes down to pain and pleasure. For instance, have you ever been at a party and been attracted to someone? You're on one end of the dance floor and this attractive person is all the way across the dance floor on the other side.

Suddenly you get the nerve to speak to that person. You start making your way across the room. You're excited. Thoughts of pleasure fill your mind as you dream about dancing with that good-looking person. After a few more steps .....all of a sudden, BAM! You stop. A little voice inside says, "Am I crazy? That person is too beautiful and too popular to dance with me. I'm just going to get rejected. And I know I can't deal with that pain."

Now what do you do? Do you let the possible pain of rejection win out and turn you around, afraid to ask for a dance? Or do you squash the thought of rejection with your excitement and desire for pleasure? What do you do?

Life is Full of Choices!

If you stop and turn around, it means that the possible pain of rejection was greater than the potential pleasure of dancing. However, if you continue moving forward to ask this attractive person to dance, it means that the potential pleasure cancelled out the possible pain.

Avoiding pain and seeking pleasure dictates most of our actions. Think about it! "What clothes did you CHOOSE to wear today?" Isn't there some pleasure you got from wearing those particular "threads"? Or did you CHOOSE those clothes to avoid the pain and ridicule from your friends for wearing out-of-style clothes?

I have come to realize that my life has turned out the way it has because of my personal choices and decisions. And the same is true for you. You are where you are today because of the choices and decisions you made yesterday. And guess what? You can predict where you'll be tomorrow or even next year by analyzing the choices and decisions you make today.

Look at it like this: You're in a maze. Your dreams and goals are at the end of this maze. Your goal may be to: raise a family, have peace of mind, become a millionaire or make our world a better place for all people. Perhaps it's a combination of many things. Whatever your goals are, the only way to reach them is to make wise choices and decisions today.

Every day, you face hundreds of choices, without always being sure of the outcome. There you are: Your heart is thumping. Thoughts flash across your mind. "Will this bring me closer to my dreams or farther away?" Fearful thoughts of pain are tangled with pleasurable emotions. You can make only one choice and with that particular choice, there will be certain consequences. There's no escape. You must deal with the consequences of your decisions. KA-BOOM, you make a decision.

INTRO

Life is Full of Choices!

You now find yourself in another room with more doors and more choices. BAM! You have to make new decisions. Again, based on those decisions you will find yourself faced with a new set of doors from which to choose.

You choose to either get out of bed when the alarm clock goes off or hit the snooze button and sleep for another hour. Now sometimes, the choice is not always yours. If your parents are like mine, they'll scream and shout to wake you up! So now you're up. Next, you come to another set of doors from which to choose. What clothes do you wear? BAM! You've decided. You finally reach school and it's time to choose between having fun with your friends or listening to your teacher in the classroom.

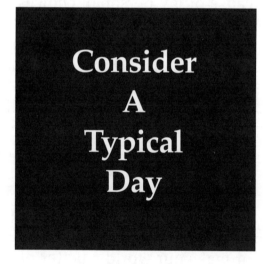

Consider A Typical Day

The maze continues. With your friends, do you choose to make fun of that nerdy student who turned in his homework or do you turn in your completed homework? When you get home, do you complete your studies or stay on the telephone? Later that evening, do you ask the person to whom you're attracted to go on a date or do you just daydream? Do you do your chores or complain about not receiving an allowance? Do you join the gang or stand alone?

Life is Full of Choices!

Life is full of choices, decisions and consequences. Right now, you are where you are because of the choices you made yesterday, last week or even last year. And check this out: the decisions you make today will influence where you end up tomorrow, next week or even next year.

So what are you going to do?
**Your life is
your responsibility.**
It's in your hands.
Will you choose to be successful
or will you, by default, choose to fail?
What is it going to be?
It's your choice!

Your **life** is your responsibility

Life is Full of Choices!

The great thing about understanding the "Maze of Life" is that you realize your past is in the past. You can't change it. But starting today, you can create an exciting future!

Unfortunately, many students do not realize how important their decisions are in determining their future. For example, all of my friends talked about going to college. Some said they were going to be the college football or basketball superstar. Others said they would be rich and famous after graduating from college. However, when it came time for our high school graduation, only a few of us actually received a diploma and went on to college.

Why is it that some of us went to college while others did not even graduate from high school?

My friends who didn't attend college were not stupid. In fact, some of them were as bright or brighter than those of us who went to college.

So what makes the difference? Why is it that one student attends college while his or her best friend drops out of high school? The answer is simple. Each student CHOOSES to make different decisions. Although most of my friends talked about going to college, there were some students who CHOSE to play around in class rather than listen to the teacher. They chose not to do their homework. They chose not to study. And as a consequence, their grades prevented them from attending college. Their dream was crushed, but it all could have been avoided if they had taken the time to seriously consider their education. Unfortunately, they did not realize how their decisions would impact their future.

Luckily for me, my life changed for the better after understanding the "Maze of Life." Today, I am empowered because I understand that every decision I make leads to "real" consequences which affect my future. I now think before I act. I know there are consequences connected to each door in this maze called "Life." Before making a choice, I ask myself, "Will this decision bring me closer to my dreams or farther away?" And based on the answer, I know what choice to make. Today, my life has taken on new meaning. And the same will happen for you.

Just by making new choices and decisions, your life will take on new meaning as you move closer to making your dreams come true.

Success Destiny

Take a close look at yourself in this maze called "Life." You are where you are today because of past decisions and choices. In this maze, you are trying to reach a destination called "success." Success means different things to different people.

Take ten minutes and write out what success means to you. Really think about it before you write. There are no right or wrong answers so just honestly write down what it would take for you to consider yourself to be successful.

To me success means:

_____

_____

_____

_____

_____

_____

_____

_____

_____

_____

You can't change your past decisions. Nor can you change your actions of the past.

But there is great news! You can learn from your past and make better decisions today.

So now you have identified what success means to you. This is your success destiny. By understanding your dreams and goals, you now realize why you have to make "good" choices and decisions every day. But before you can actually achieve your goals, you must believe that you can do it, or else, you will probably sabotage your own success. **In the blank space found inside the maze, write down all your reasons why you will claim success and happiness.**

I will achieve my goals and fulfill my dreams because:

© Success By Choice, 1993 • (510) 887-1311

Success Destiny

Now you realize that you can achieve your goals and fulfill your dreams. By staying focused on your goals, your daily journey within this maze called "Life" will be truly exciting as you move closer to your destiny of success. However, let me ask you a serious question: Have your decisions and choices of last year, or last month, or last week or even yesterday put you on the right path to reach your goals and dreams? Perhaps they have, perhaps they haven't. But it really doesn't matter now. The past is in the past. Don't punish yourself for something you did in the past. Just learn from it and grow. Today is a new day!

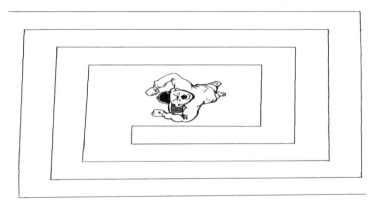

If you were heading down the wrong path or made some decisions that you regret, not all is lost. Starting today, just make wise decisions that will put you back on a path to success. Understand this: We are all human and we do make mistakes from time to time. And when this happens, the most important thing to do is learn from your mistake and move on. **The key to success is to learn from your mistakes or "bad" decisions and move on.** As long as you learn a lesson, you grow. And if you grow, you become a wiser person. By learning lessons, you will make better decisions in the "Maze of Life." And by making better decisions, you will not encounter as many difficult consequences along your journey to success.

The **Key** to **Success** is to learn from your mistakes or "bad" decisions and **Move On!**

Where Are You Going With *Your* Life?

Success Destiny

Write down three mistakes that you have made in the past.

1. _____
_____
2. _____
_____
3. _____
_____

As a result of those decisions, write down the consequences that you encountered.

1. _____
_____
2. _____
_____
3. _____
_____

Now, write down the lessons that you have learned from experiencing those mistakes.

1. _____
_____
2. _____
_____
3. _____
_____

If you faced those exact three situations again, what decisions would you make today?

1. _____
_____
2. _____
_____
3. _____
_____

By learning lessons from your mistakes, you Grow!

And by growing, you move closer to YOUR SUCCESS DESTINY.

The "Maze of Life" is Very Real

Congratulations, you have written your thoughts regarding what success means as well as some lessons you've learned from past mistakes. Now that you know where you're heading, take a closer look at the "Maze of Life" and picture yourself before it, preparing to make decisions before each door. Your success destiny represents some of your goals and dreams. But remember, in order for you to reach this destiny, you must make good decisions in the various rooms of this maze called "Life."

INTRO

The "Maze of Life" is Very Real

Each room can either help you reach your dreams or block you from moving forward. This is why it is so important to THINK and make wise choices before taking action. The door you choose in each room is critical to your success. To see how you deal with certain choices, let's now consider some of the rooms in the "Maze of Life."

There you are. You walk into a room labeled "education." Regarding the choice of **obtaining an education**, which door do you choose?

Door #1: Do you strive to be recognized as the class clown enjoying the laughter of your classmates and disrupting the learning process?

Door #2: Do you do just enough to get a passing grade or try to "get over" by copying your classmate's test?

Door #3: Do you work, listen, do all assignments, ask questions and apply yourself, striving to receive all "A's" and "B's"?

What door have you opened? Write the door number which you have chosen today. _____
Is the answer as obvious to you as it was to me? If you have thought about what we've been discussing, and remember your success destiny, then Door #3 was your choice. If you did not pick Door #3, then talk about your choice with someone whom you respect. Now proceed to the room labeled "Sex."

The "Maze of Life" is Very Real

Door #1:
Do you abstain and wait to have sex when you are married?

Door #2:
Do you have sex with everyone that you can?

Door #3:
Do you have sex with only that "special" someone?

What door have you opened? Write the door number which you have chosen today.

Some choices lead to pain while others lead to pleasure. And in some cases, people choose a particular door for the short-term pleasure, not considering the long-term impact of pain. For instance, some people get caught up in their emotions and have sex without any protection. They are only focusing on the short-term pleasure. They don't consider the life-changing effects of teen pregnancy or the very real danger of contracting AIDS. Now that you've made your decision, let's keep moving. You next enter a room labeled "Drugs."

The "Maze of Life" is Very Real

This is no joke! There are decisions and choices to make every day. One wrong choice could kill you or someone else. For instance, everyday, there are stories of people who are killed in automobile accidents caused by drivers under the influence of drugs or alcohol. In each case, the driver made a choice. Unfortunately, this choice made the difference between life and death.

Our choices and decisions will ultimately bring happiness or sadness. Although it is our personal choices and decisions that affect the quality of our lives, we can sometimes be influenced by someone or something. In fact, all of us are influenced. Remember how I was influenced by my instigating friends to fight Paul in school?

So what is the major influence in your life? Maybe that influence is your parents, a six-pack of beer, your friends, money, television, the local gang, a celebrity or God.

Write down the major influences in your life.

_____

_____

_____

_____

Are these influences having a positive or negative impact upon your life? Please explain.

_____

_____

_____

_____

In regard to the choice of drinking alcohol and doing drugs, which door do you choose?

Door #1:
Do you choose the door labeled "Never"?

Door #2:
Do you choose the door labeled "Occasionally"?

Door #3:
Do you choose the door labeled "Whenever I can"?

Regarding drugs, what door have you opened? Write the door number which you have chosen today.

Do not ever let a mistake knock you down and keep you down.

Remember this: When you get knocked down by life, pray that you land on your back because if you can look up, you can get up!

Learn a lesson, make new plans and move on.

The "Maze of Life" is Very Real

Many influences have played major roles in my life. Some of my influences were negative. And as a result, I made morally distasteful decisions which restricted my future. Hopefully, as I share some of my experiences, you will learn from my mistakes so that you will not have to experience the same consequences.

Although you and I are not exactly alike, there is much you'll learn from reading my story. Our definition of success is not identical. In fact, everyone has a different perspective of success. Remember how you wrote your thoughts regarding success?

That's the beauty of life. Each of us is different and unique. No matter what your dreams or goals may be, you can do it! It's just a matter of making certain decisions that move you closer to your dreams. If you happen to make a wrong decision or a mistake, don't worry. It's not the end of the world. We all make mistakes. Nobody is perfect. Even you will make some mistakes from time to time. That's just life.

However, the key to success is to learn lessons from your mistakes and move on!

The "Maze of Life" is Very Real

Before we move on, keep in mind that your future is in your own hands. Repeat ten times out loud, "My success is my choice." Stand up! Get ready. Get set. Go!

This is for real! Today is the start of your successful journey through this maze called "Life." Claim your success as you move closer to your goals and dreams. Your success destiny can become a reality. It can definitely happen. But it's up to you, and ONLY YOU. Sure, others (your parents, friends, teachers and family) can support you, but you have to take responsibility for your own life. Make your dreams come true. You can do it. Today is a new day. Yesterday is gone. And no matter what's happened to you in the past, today is a new day. Remember, your choices and decisions made today will directly impact where you'll be tomorrow.

This maze called **"Life"** has many doors, many paths and many consequences. Take responsibility for your life and think first before you act. Remember, there are consequences to face after each decision you make. Negative consequences could turn into roadblocks. And these roadblocks can make it more difficult for you in achieving your goals. In some instances, these roadblocks could ultimately prevent you from ever reaching your goals (i.e., lifelong drug addiction or life-term prison sentence).

The "Maze of Life" is Very Real

Although any one roadblock could prevent you from reaching your destiny, this book includes insight as to how you can overcome a few roadblocks in particular.

In this book, I share my experiences with you so that you can avoid making some of the mistakes that I've made. I also share SUCCESS KEYS for overcoming various roadblocks. With these success keys, you will be able to unlock more doors of opportunity as you move forward on your journey through this maze called "Life."

As you can see, this is an exciting opportunity. However, the true power lies in your hands. As you read this book, you will discover many different situations with just as many different responses. While reading, think about how you would handle each particular situation. You will have the opportunity to write your ideas and thoughts to various questions. Do not just read this book and over look the questions. You will be empowered when you answer these questions. Get involved and get the most from this book. By answering these questions and actively participating in the various exercises, your life will take on new meaning. Don't miss this opportunity to unleash your true potential to the world.

The "Maze of Life" is Very Real

So What's The Answer to Success And Happiness?

What is the answer? Well, first of all, realize that you're not alone. That's what this book is all about. In fact, don't just think of this as just another book. It's more of a guide through this maze called "Life." This book discusses various issues of life ranging from self-esteem to peer pressure to your education.

In this guide, my friends and I share our experiences. And because we have already gone through what you're presently going through or soon to face, our suggestions can help you deal successfully with the various issues in your life. Read each page carefully and absorb the wisdom distilled in the sentences. However, to reap the most from this book, I suggest you write down your answers to all the questions. When you put your thoughts on paper, you can see them and they become more clear. Something magical occurs when we write our thoughts on paper. With this commitment, your life will have more focus. You will also begin to recognize your true potential.

So please write your thoughts and complete the various exercises throughout this book. By doing this, you will definitely be empowered. Your journey through life will become easier as you overcome the various roadblocks that pop up in life.

By reading each chapter, you will be empowered with success keys. As you read my story, you will also discover and appreciate your potential. If you answer the questions and implement the various success techniques presented here, your cries for help will be answered. You will develop some new practices that will empower your life. And that's a blessing!

Let's now move on by reading the next chapter and see how I handle the first roadblock to success known as "Suffering From Low Self-Esteem and Lacking Self-Confidence."

It's 6:30, Friday morning. I'm at home. I'm feeling depressed. I'm hurting! Turn to the next page and see how you can also overcome this first roadblock to success.

Let's agree that **you will take time to answer the questions and write your answers in this book. Just do it!**

I (Name) _____ pledge to read this entire book from beginning to end, answer all questions throughout and practice each exercise.

Signature _____ Today's Date _____

It's 6:30, Friday morning.

I'm in my bedroom lying in bed. It's been a long night. I'm not feeling very happy. In fact, I feel miserable. I don't even want to get out of bed. I'd rather just pull the covers up over my head and sleep the day away. You see, at this moment, I'm not feeling very confident. To be honest, I've been feeling sad for a long time. Not much is going right in my life:

I'm failing in school.
   I don't have many friends.
      My parents are always blaming me.
      Everyone's on my back.
        I'm fat.
        I'm ugly.
          I have too many pimples.
          My life is boring....

I don't want to see anybody today. I can no longer cover my pain with the fake smiles.

To escape reality, I'll just pull the covers over my head and sleep the day away.

I Want to HIDE! HIDE! HIDE! HIDE! HIDE!

Have you ever had a similar experience?

Are you happy right now?

What a question, huh?

Unfortunately, many of us are not as happy as we could be. In fact, some people are too hard on themselves. They are their own worst critics. I know what it's like, I've been there. That's how it used to be for me. I used to beat myself up. I was always complaining about the things going wrong in my life. I just overlooked all the positive things in my life. I was very hard on myself. I complained about everything and everyone. I felt sorry for myself. Basically, I was not happy.

In my school, clothes were very important. The most popular students wore the latest style fashions. In fact, many students would rush to the store to buy similar "threads" worn by their favorite movie stars and entertainers. Each week, kids would show-off their new clothes and receive many compliments. The clothes that you wore were a big deal.

Like all students, I wanted to be popular and wear the designer clothes, too. But unfortunately, my family didn't have much money. In fact, I'll never forget approaching my mom about buying the latest name brand tennis shoes for me. Many months passed and she had the exact same response:

"Nolram, we don't have that type of money. We're barely making it. I'm just trying to make sure we have enough food on the table for you, your sisters and brothers. We don't have $150 for a pair of tennis shoes."

One night after dinner, I shouted, "Come on, mom, everyone is wearing the latest-style shoes. My friends laugh at the shoes that I wear. I want to be accepted. I don't want them laughing at me."

She didn't respond. In the silence that followed, I wasn't sure what was going to happen next.

With tears swelling up in her eyes, she said, "Nolram, happiness and joy do not depend on what you wear or own, but rather on how you feel from within. These so-called friends who judge the shoes that you wear are not worth calling real friends. One day, you'll understand that you've got too many positive things in your life to be focused on those things that really don't matter. I love you Nolram and will always love you regardless of what type of shoes you're wearing. But you have to have this same unconditional love for yourself. One day, you'll understand."

She then kissed me on the cheek and marched off into her bedroom.

I thought to myself, "What does she mean? I'm not really sure what she means, but I know one thing for sure — I still don't have those $150 tennis shoes."

I know what will make me HAPPY! It's Those $150 Tennis Shoes

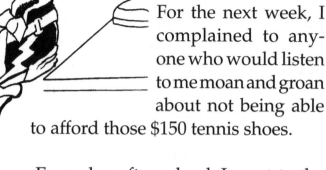

For the next week, I complained to anyone who would listen to me moan and groan about not being able to afford those $150 tennis shoes.

Everyday after school, I went to the athletic store in the mall. I stared at the rainbow of colored tennis shoes on the shelves. I would just fantasize and drool over my favorite pair of dream shoes. It became an obsession. This continued for many weeks until one day my life changed. I'll never forget it.

I was at the athletic store, again, complaining about not being able to afford my dream shoes. The newest style shoes had just arrived off the truck. The store manager was stocking them on the shelves. I watched in pain, knowing that I couldn't buy them. And to make matters worst, I knew all of my friends would soon be wearing this latest pair. As thoughts of them wearing these new shoes and me wearing my old, outdated shoes grew stronger, I became more upset.

I knew I had to get away from there. I had to leave from this torture. So I finally left the store, feeling like a helpless victim. Still moaning, I made my way toward the elevator and pushed the button, all the while thinking, "It's not fair. Why me?" Time froze as I continued to complain.

ROADBLOCK

1

The elevator door finally opened. To my surprise, a guy in a wheelchair looked directly at me. I was shocked! He said in a booming voice, "Hi there, it's a great day, huh?" I couldn't answer because I was still in shock. I immediately looked down and couldn't believe what I was seeing. He had no legs. He woke me up from my daze with, "Well, are you coming in?" I nervously said, "Oh yeah,..... yeah,....... I'm going to the fourth level bus stop." With excitement, he responded, "Wonderful! Come on in." I walked in. The elevator door shut behind me.

He said, "I don't see any bags with you, did you do any shopping?" I stuttered, "Ah.......I just went to the ...um......athletic store to look at the latest-style............um...... shoes." He shouted enthusiastically, "Man, I just love those new Air-Jordans." Confused by his answer, I didn't say anything. I thought to myself, "How could he like shoes, he has no legs."

Life is great and getting better all the time!

Noticing my uneasiness, he said, "Oh, you think because I have no legs that I can't possibly be interested in tennis shoes. Well, for a long time after my accident, I was bitter and depressed and wasn't interested in *anything*, let alone shoes. But then I realized that although my legs were lost, I was still blessed with a healthy mind. To me, life is great. **And today, I choose to look at life with happy eyes rather than with sad ones.** There are too many positive things to be excited about. I decided to focus on the things that are meaningful, rather than those which don't mean anything. It's not what happens to you that's important. But rather, what's important is how you respond. Your response determines whether or not you're happy. I choose to be happy. **Life is *great* and getting better all the time!"**

I was in deep thought. I felt like a fool for complaining about what I didn't have. Here, I didn't have a pair of tennis shoes, yet this guy didn't have any legs and he was much happier than me.

DING! We had arrived at the third floor. The elevator doors opened. He enthusiastically said, "Well, here we are — third level bus stop. Have a great day. And remember to enjoy life to the fullest."

He then rolled out and waved good-bye. He said, "Bye" as the elevator door shut.

Stunned, I couldn't say anything.

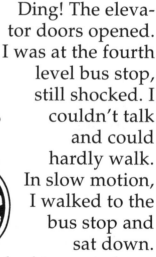

Ding! The elevator doors opened. I was at the fourth level bus stop, still shocked. I couldn't talk and could hardly walk. In slow motion, I walked to the bus stop and sat down.

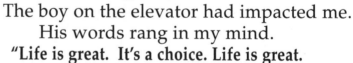

The boy on the elevator had impacted me. His words rang in my mind.
"Life is great. It's a choice. Life is great. Enjoy life to the fullest. It's a choice....Choice.....Blessed.....Life is great."
His words continued to bombard my mind. I then recalled the conversation with my mom. It was amazing. Wham! Bam! All of a sudden, I finally understood what mom was saying.

I learned the first lesson of life: **"Success and happiness come from within and not from outside forces, things or other people."**

ROADBLOCK

1

Life can be really great if we want it to be. It's all a matter of where we choose to place our focus. I was unhappy because I chose to focus on the lack in my life, and on things not going the way I wanted. However, the boy in the wheelchair chose to focus on the good in his life. Yes, happiness is certainly a choice. Do you choose to be happy? If you're not happy with your life, just try missing a day. Just the fact that you're breathing and your heart is pumping is a reason to be happy.

Happiness is

Take a few moments and write some things about your life that make you happy.

_____

_____

_____

_____

_____

_____

_____

_____

_____

_____

So I ask you again, are you happy? How are things going for you right now? I'm sure that there are many wonderful things to be happy about. And just as well, there are some areas that you would probably like to improve. So let's get busy and concentrate on those areas that you want to improve. Here is an opportunity for you to make a decision and take some action to improve the quality of your life.

a CHOICE

Suffering From

Low Self Esteem
& Lacking Self-Confidence

List ten things in your life that you want to improve or change.

1. _____
2. _____
3. _____
4. _____
5. _____
6. _____
7. _____
8. _____
9. _____
10. _____

Now, go back through the list and put a check mark by the things that you have control over and can change. For instance, you can take certain steps to change your weight, but you cannot necessarily change your height.

Now for those things over which you have control, list the five most important things that you want to improve or change. The ranking will be from one to five with one being the most important.

Write down your top five improvement areas.

1. _____
2. _____
3. _____
4. _____
5. _____

Let's now develop a plan to improve these particular areas of concern.

ROADBLOCK

1

Questions......

1. What do I need to do every single day to accomplish my goal?

2. Which individuals or groups can help me accomplish my goal?

3. What is the date by which I will have successfully accomplished my goal?

4. What are some possible roadblocks that may delay me in accomplishing my goal?

5. How will I overcome these obstacles?

These five improvement areas are now personal goals. For each of these five goals, you will write a plan as to how you will successfully accomplish that particular goal. In your plan, be sure to answer these five questions.

Write down your plan to achieve goal # 1.
_____
_____

Write down your plan to achieve goal # 2.
_____
_____

Write down your plan to achieve goal # 3.
_____
_____

Write down your plan to achieve goal # 4.
_____
_____

Write down your plan to achieve goal # 5.
_____
_____

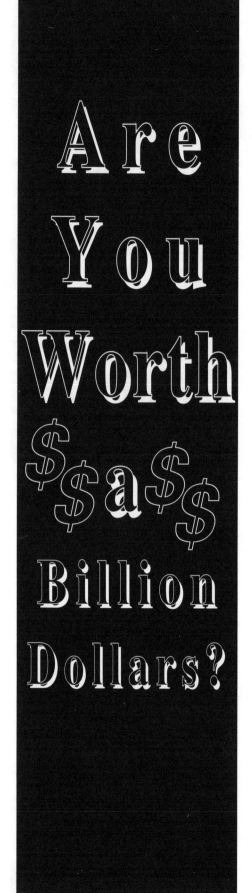

Are You Worth $$a$$ Billion Dollars?

I commend you for being proactive and taking action in developing your plan. Now you must take action and follow your plan. Many people complain and complain but never take any action. They ultimately end up doing the same things over and over again. It's crazy. They continue to do things that keep them from achieving their goals. But you are different. You are taking action and successfully moving closer to achieving your goals. Congratulations! You are now in the process of overcoming some personal concerns of the past. By working on your top five improvement areas, you are walking on a path that is bringing you closer to your dreams.

Wonderful! You are now working on some improvement areas. But let's not forget that you're already magnificently blessed. At this very moment, there are many wonderful things in your life. Remember, happiness is a choice. It depends on where you focus your attention.

For instance, did you know that you're literally worth a billion dollars?

You're probably thinking to yourself, "Nolram is crazy." I know, it might sound farfetched. But wait until you realize what I've learned about you. Check it out:

Your brain is a magnificent gift. And just think, you were born with it. In terms of intricacy and power, it outperforms even the greatest modern computer technology. Your brain is capable of processing up to 30 billion bits of information per second and boasts the equivalent of 6,000 miles of wiring and cabling. In numerical form, a million is written down as: 1,000,000. In numerical form, write down what 30 billion looks like in this space. _____

30 billion bits ....WOW! That's amazing. Can you believe it? It's a huge number, huh? It's a gigantic number. And just think, your brain can process this number of bits of information EACH SECOND. Isn't that incredible?

But hold on, we're not finished yet. There's more to you.......

ROADBLOCK
1

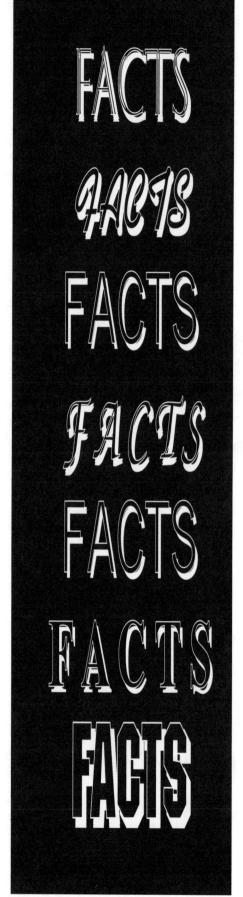

Your human nervous system contains approximately 28 billion neurons (nerve cells designed to conduct impulses). These neurons allow you to interpret information received through your sense organs. They also allow for instructions from your brain to be carried out. Each of these neurons is a tiny, self-contained computer capable of processing about one million bits of information.

These neurons act independently, but they also communicate with other neurons through an amazing network of 100,000 miles of nerve fibers. Can you believe it? There is 100,000 miles of nerve fibers in your body. That's right, in your body. Just imagine, 100,000 miles, that would be the equivalent to driving thirty times across the United States, from the East Coast to the West Coast.

A reaction in one neuron can spread to hundreds of thousands of others in a span of less than twenty milliseconds. Blink your eyes right now. To give you perspective on how fast twenty milliseconds is, it's about ten times less than it takes for your eyes to blink. Now that's fast!

Put your hand over your heart. Do you feel it beating? Just think for a moment. It's operating for you. And you don't even have to consciously monitor or control each beat. And thank God! Could you imagine how it would be if you forgot to continue the beating for just ten seconds? Your oversight could be a deathly mistake. Your heart pumps about 63 gallons of blood every hour. Did you know that? You are magnificent! But let's not stop yet.

Every day, you breathe approximately 2,500 gallons of air to supply your tissues with oxygen. Now 2,500 gallons is a lot. How many twelve ounce cans of your favorite soda would be required to equal 2,500 gallons?....

Now, that's a lot of oxygen. And you need all 2,500 gallons of oxygen every day. Without oxygen, cells become weak and die. There are an estimated 50 trillion cells in your body. This is about 10,000 times the Earth's present population.

...Answer Here...

During this upcoming week, take time to read some books and discover more amazing things about yourself. **Be sure to write down five of your new discoveries here, and then share your discoveries with your friends and family.**

1._____

2._____

3._____

4._____

5._____

Hopefully, we now agree that you are wonderfully made. Do you realize how much potential you have? No matter what has happened to you in the past, tomorrow is a new day. In fact, you are literally not the same person that you were last year. Did you know that ninety-eight percent of the atoms in your body were not there a year ago? Hard to believe, huh? Well, continue reading.

Your skeleton that seems so solid was not there three months ago. The configuration of your bone cells remains somewhat constant, but atoms of all kinds pass freely back and forth through the cell walls, and that means you acquire a new skeleton every three months. Your skin is new every month. You have a new stomach lining every four days, with the actual surface cells that contact food being renewed every five minutes. The cells in the liver turn over very slowly, but new atoms still flow through them, like water in a river course, making a new liver every six weeks.

As you can see, you are literally changing from within everyday. You don't have to do anything to change the insides of your body. It happens automatically. However, it takes a conscious decision to change your thoughts. Remember, happiness is a choice. You can either focus on the positive or the negative issues in your life. It's a choice. With all this immense power at our disposal, why can't we get ourselves to feel happy each and every day? There are many reasons. I know, I've been there. One reason is that we sometimes overlook the many blessings in our life. Remember the feelings I described at the beginning of this chapter? I was sad. However today, instead of feeling miserable, I am excited about life and who I am. You also can recognize your many blessings. In fact, I've got a suggestion.

Let's now focus on the positive. Take five minutes and write down the blessings in your life. Write down the things that make you happy. You have five minutes. Write down as many positive blessings as fast as you can. Write down everything you like about yourself. Include all your achievements, awards and contributions. Write down anything that makes you proud. Get ready, get set, GO!

_____

_____

_____

_____

_____

_____

_____

_____

_____

_____

_____

_____

_____

How do you feel? Did you know that you had so many blessings? Now you realize that there are many blessings in your life. Isn't life great? You have so much of which to be proud. I am sure that you want to continue this positive feeling. But how will you continue feeling good about yourself all the time?

The following two exercises have helped change my attitude from being sad about life to being excited about life. If you do these exercises every day, you will feel better. In fact, your life will take on new meaning.

Exercise #1:
Every morning and every night after brushing your teeth, look into the bathroom mirror. Look directly into your eyes and repeat aloud the following statements.

"I'm beautiful. I'm smart. No one is exactly like me, I'm a miracle. I'm great just the way I am. I've got a bright future. Life is great. I love you."

Now blow a kiss to yourself in the mirror. I know it seems silly, but it works. You will start appreciating yourself more. Give it a try. Commit to doing this each morning and every night for one complete week. It's only seven days. Make the commitment, you're definitely worth it. Believe me, it works if you work it. Just do it! Seven days straight. For the next seven days, write down each time you do this exercise.

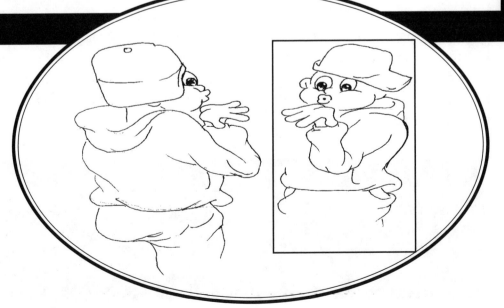

Exercise #2:

You are successful every day. Remember, it's just a matter of recognizing those positive things in your life. To recognize your accomplishments of the day, start writing in a success journal. This is similar to a diary. However, it's more than a diary because it highlights ONLY successful accomplishments and positive things that make you proud and happy. Commit to writing at least one accomplishment in your success journal before you go to bed each night. If you have more than one accomplishment, that's great. Write all of your achievements in your success journal. By doing this every night, you will realize that each day was a true success. You will sleep much better. Remember, even if things don't go as planned, as long as you can learn a lesson, you have grown. And by growing, you become a wiser person. In your success journal, record all the lessons that you have learned.

Once I began writing in a success journal, my life took on new meaning. Today, I feel better about myself. And the same will happen for you. By recognizing your achievements and accomplishments, your life will become more fulfilling. You will achieve more goals. You will be happier. In fact, you may even sleep with a smile on your face.

You are successful everyday...
Just recognize it!

These two exercises are just tools to help you look within yourself and realize your true unlimited strength. Your strength actually comes to you from generations of people who overcame tremendous obstacles of the past.

Have you ever thought about the people who came over from Africa in twenty-pound shackles, lying at the bottom of slave ships? Do you realize the strength and faith it took to survive such a horrible trip? And those African slaves who did survive encountered terrible experiences here in America, first as slaves, and later as freed men and women who really didn't have true freedom. They did, however, overcome many obstacles: lynching, segregation, poverty, and injustice. We can learn from their perseverance. They kept their eyes on the prize and pushed for true justice.

WHO ARE YOU?

DO YOU KNOW?

Think, for a moment, about the early people who came to this country and weathered many hardships. Or what about the millions of Jews who overcame the Holocaust less than a century ago? The odds were against all of these people but they persisted and overcame challenging trials and tribulations. And what about the Japanese whose cities were destroyed in bombings during World War II? They chose to not lie down and cry. But rather, they picked themselves up and rebuilt their cities.

The main point is that we all come from strong people. Your grandparents and great grandparents were powerful people. Think about your roots and ask yourself: **"Do I know who I really am? Do I know the true strength of those who made certain choices so that I could be here today?"**

Your past is rooted in the spirits of strong individuals who fought so that you *could* be here today. That persistence continues in people that we see around us today. Take an incident close to home, for example. Think about a time when your family came together and persisted to overcome a major challenge. Maybe, it was when a major appliance broke at your home. Your parents didn't really have the money to get it fixed, but something needed to be done. You may have seen your father take on an extra job, or your mom work overtime to make the extra money to get it fixed. Maybe a grandmother, uncle or cousin came up with the money and gave it to your family.

This is only an example, but you can probably recall many times when you witnessed or experienced the satisfaction of overcoming various obstacles. Why don't you take some time now to remember a few situations where you saw your family's strength in action? Or, what about a time when you saw a group of people or an individual overcome obstacles and roadblocks that seemed far too great?

Take a few moments and write five examples of when you or someone close to you accomplished something that seemed impossible:

1. _____

_____

_____

_____

2. _____

_____

_____

_____

_____

3. _____

_____

_____

_____

_____

4. _____

_____

_____

_____

5. _____

_____

_____

_____

So there it is. You have witnessed real-life scenarios of acheivement.
By acquiring this same mindset, you too, will achieve.
Remember, you are on your way
to success and happiness.

Do you remember your first roller coaster ride?
I sure remember mine. In fact, I'll never forget how my friend Jerome convinced me to ride.

" I can't wait to ride on that roller coaster."

"Oh boy, look at that long line. I don't want to wait for hours in that line."

" Look man, this is supposed to be the scariest roller coaster ride in the park. We're not going home until we ride this. Come on now, Nolram, you're not a wimp, right?"

" OK, I'll ride!"

What was your first roller coaster ride like? Was it like this?

Your heart was beating with excitement on one beat and thumping with fear on the next. It was thrilling! After the safety guard locked you into your seat, you thought, "Do I really want to do this?" But before you could answer, the train started moving. There was no turning back now.

Oh, no, now the train is moving slowly up that big hill. You hear the sound "Click, click, click, click, click." You're thinking, "I can't believe I'm here." People on the ground are looking smaller and smaller, becoming the size of ants. You're getting dizzy, feeling like you may throw-up. WHAM! The train finally makes it to the top of that gigantic hill. Wooooooooooooosssh! The train goes flying down the hill, upside down, up and down, up and down. People are screaming. You're thinking, "When will this end?" as you're jerked to the left and pushed up against your friend seated next to you. As the train comes off that huge hill it slows down. Everyone sighs in relief. It's finally over. You're exhausted. Some people are laughing and saying, "That was great." Others are crying, "That was terrible. Let me off. I don't want to ever do that again."

What are you saying?

Life

An Emotional Roller Coaster!

Why is it that two people can experience the exact same thing, but have two absolutely different responses? It makes you think, huh?

Life is similar to a roller coaster ride: There are many ups and downs. There are even times when you're upside down. There are periods when you feel excited. But also, there are times when you feel you have no control. You feel like you're at the mercy of outside forces.

Like many people, I see my own life as an emotional roller coaster. Like that small train moving up the incline in one moment then taking the ultimate drop in the next, there are times when either I'm confidently on top of the world, or at the bottom, crying on my knees for life to stop being so cruel.

Yes, we're talking about the same ride, one filled with many emotions: fear, excitement, confusion, happiness, depression, confidence and terror.

They are all wrapped up in a roller coaster ride called *Life*

44

WHY?
WHY?
WHY?
WHY?
WHY?
WHY?
WHY?
WHY
ME??
?????

Is this how your life has been? Are you up some-times? Down at other times? If you answer yes, you can probably relate to what I'm saying.

You may be asking yourself, "How can this author relate to me?" Well, like you, I sat through some boring classes, had some teachers I couldn't stand, cheered for my favorite football and basketball teams, got butterflies when approaching my sweetheart, partied at school dances and, last but certainly not least, complained about my restrictive parents.

I can even remember some hardships in which I went as far as questioning God by saying, "Why me?" Sometimes it was very difficult. Tears flowed down my face as I cried out for help. Many times I felt as if I was at the bottom of the roller coaster.

But just like the roller coaster ride, I made it through. And so will you.

IT'S NOT THE END OF THE WORLD!

No matter what you're experiencing, it's not the end of the world. We all experience crushing trials and tribulations that force us to our knees as we cry out for help. Many of us have felt alone at times as we experience some difficult challenge. For example :

- I remember how sad I was when my first girlfriend told me that she wanted to end our relationship. I broke down. To me, it was the end of the world.

- Tom, a friend, shared with me how he practiced day and night to be selected to play on his high school varsity basketball team. He cried for days after finding out that he had been cut from the team.

- Sharon experienced ridicule for being slightly overweight. Her "friends" made jokes about her. Jokes like, "What weighs 200 pounds and doesn't move too fast?" appeared to be funny at the time. But it scarred Sharon for life and crippled her confidence.

- Jason wanted to become an artist but his parents pushed him to become a doctor. He hates his medical profession. Today, he's unhappy because he's not fulfilling his God-blessed mission of painting beautiful pictures.

- Christina was definitely in the in-crowd. She was very popular in school. Unfortunately, she got caught up in the fast life and didn't apply herself in school. She failed to graduate, and now, she can't get a job that pays enough to take care of her children.

- Albert was into expensive clothes. He always had the "best." He wore expensive jewelry, the latest name-brand tennis shoes and designer shirts. Everyone admired him; he was "The Man." Unfortunately, he thought more about making fast money than obtaining an education. He dropped out of school and started selling drugs. One day a deal went bad. He was shot four times. He was later arrested and convicted. He is now serving a thirty-four-year sentence in prison.

THIS TOO SHALL PASS!

The list goes on and on. Many friends have shared countless experiences and horror stories about their lives. So, no matter what you're going through, don't worry, because *"This too shall pass."* Think about your current challenge and shout aloud, *"This too shall pass."*

Many people have overcome great challenges in their lives, some of whom are well-known celebrities. For instance, did you know:

Michael Jordan tried out for the varsity basketball team in his high school and was not picked to play on the team when he first tried out but was rather cut from the team.

Oprah Winfrey grew up in a poor family. She was sexually abused and rebelled by taking part in acts of delinquency.

It's hard to believe that today's hottest and most popular celebrities have encountered their share of difficult challenges. But they have. Many have beaten the odds. Some were told that they would never amount to anything. Fortunately, they did not listen to those negative people and proved them wrong. You and I can learn from their example of perseverance. Check out this commitment:

- He failed at business at age 21.
- He was defeated in a legislative race at age 22.
- He failed again in business at age 24.
- He overcame the death of his sweetheart at age 26.
- He had a nervous breakdown at age 27.
- He lost a congressional race at age 34.
- He lost another congressional race at age 36.
- He lost a senatorial race at age 45.
- He failed in an effort to become vice president at age 47.
- He lost another senatorial race at age 49.
- He was elected president of the United States at age 52.

Now that is commitment. Guess who it is? The man's name is Abraham Lincoln.

No matter what you're going through, you will make it. Whenever I encounter a difficult challenge, I say to myself, over and over again, *"This too shall pass."* Remember, every night-time of darkness is followed by a day of sunshine. And every roller coaster ride has ups and downs. Always remember, each *down* is followed by an *up.*

In fact, there were times in my life when everything appeared to be wonderful. However, these great times of being "up" could not cover-up the many "down" periods of being depressed and unhappy.

At times, life became truly unbearable. I felt like I was lifting a five-hundred-pound weight. I was extremely unhappy and wanted to end my vicious ride on this emotional roller coaster. At times like these, the world seemed so overpowering and difficult.

I'm sure you've had days when life seemed to take you through some *serious changes*. Problems seem to get a hold of you, strangle your thoughts, and not let go. For instance, maybe you and your boyfriend just broke up. Or it could be that you've just failed a test. Maybe your parents are constantly hassling and punishing you. Or it could be that peer pressure is hurting you. Your friends just don't seem to understand what you're going through.

For most kids your age, and even adults, life is a series of many "ups" and "downs." Some people choose to view their lives as characterized by those "down" periods of depression, frustration and sadness.

Yes, I must say that I've had many low points in my life. However, I have changed my thoughts from being sad to being excited about who I really am. I now look at life as an exciting adventure. Life is no longer simply a series of "ups" and "downs."

Of course, I still face challenges, obstacles, fears, trials and tribulations. They haven't disappeared. The "downs" will always be there. Yet, I have changed my outlook on life. I no longer view myself as a helpless victim. I now perceive the "downs" as an opportunity for growth. And because of this revelation, my life has been truly blessed. These low points are really opportunities for you and me to learn a valuable lesson of life.

It's similar to a math teacher giving you homework "problems" to solve. By working through the problems, you learn how to use the math lesson in solving for the answer. And this is true of life: full of "problems" for you to solve. What you'll soon begin to realize is that these problems are just learning opportunities in disguise. So get excited!

You may be saying to yourself, "Nolram, I agreed with you so far. But now, you've totally lost it. These low periods are exciting times? I just don't buy that." Well, I definitely can understand your perspective. But just give me a chance. Let me share two reasons why these low points are really exciting.

First, by dealing with the various challenges of life, you grow and become a better person. My new philosophy is, "Everything happens for a reason and it happens to benefit me. I am no longer a victim. I am no longer a chicken, but rather a conqueror!" As I said before, everyday, you encounter challenges, obstacles, fears, trials and tribulations. They will always exist. And as long as they do, so does your opportunity for more learning and growth!

Everything happens for a reason...

You are no longer a Prisoner of your Past! But rather, you are a Pioneer of your Future!

Second, by experiencing hardships, the next low period will not be as painful as the previous one, because you have learned something. For example, have you ever made the mistake of touching a hot pot on the stove? I remember when I did. I screamed because I got burned. Now that's a lesson neither one of us needs to learn a second time.

By learning new lessons, growth and maturity take you to a higher level of consciousness. You pass the test. You advance to the next grade level. As a result of learning lessons, your roller coaster ride becomes an upward progression.

Because I maintain this philosophy in my life, I am no longer crying. My friends and I have squashed the random thoughts of being victims. We now assume responsibility for everything that happens in our lives. Today, we choose to focus on the positive things in our lives. There are still "problems" that we face each day. But now, we have the confidence that we'll make it through these potential roadblocks because we have surpassed many challenges in the past. And just think, you have also overcome many trials and tribulations in your life. You continue to learn from your past decisions and move on because you realize that tomorrow is a new day. Stay confident and make positive things happen. You can do it because you have so much potential. You are claiming your future and moving closer towards making your dreams come true.

As you remember, at 6:30 this morning, I was not feeling too happy. I didn't want to get out of bed because I was feeling sad. But I feel better now. I've overcome the first roadblock, known as "Suffering From Low Self-Esteem and Lacking Confidence." Let's now move on and discuss various success keys to help you open up more doors of opportunity.

No Matter what others think,

Becoming Clear on Your Goals

I walked into the kitchen singing, "With God on my side, I can do ALL things."

Mom asked, "So what do you want to be when you grow up?"

Caught off-guard, I replied, "Um,............I'm not sure. But I'm dreaming."

Success Keys
Are you still dreaming? What are some of your dreams? Answer here.
_____
_____
_____

Remember as little kids how we used to say, "I'm gonna be an astronaut"?
"Well, I'm gonna be a fireman."
"Well, I'm gonna be president of the United States!"
"WOOOOOOOOOOOOOOOW"

Are you still dreaming? Or are society, your family and friends strangling and choking your dreams?

When I was younger, many of my friends put me down. Whenever I shared my dreams with them, they just laughed at me. Many friends told me that my dreams would never come true. Has this ever happened to you? Do your friends build you up or break you down? Are they really "true" friends who support you?

Realize this: no matter what others think, the most important opinion regarding your life is your opinion. I've changed my dreams many times from wanting to become an astronaut, to a singer, to a professional football player, and even to a writer. I've had so many interests because I've spent long hours thinking about my life and where my future was heading. My suggestion for you is to take some time TODAY to think about your life and where you're heading.

the most important opinion regarding your life is your opinion.

The first thing to do is get clear on what makes you happy. What really gets you excited about life? By answering the following questions, you will gain valuable insight and direction for your life. These questions may be some of the most important questions which you will ever answer.

In your life, what is most important to you?

_____

_____

_____

_____

_____

_____

If you had three wishes, what would they be? And do not write 'more wishes.'

1._____

_____

2._____

_____

3._____

_____

What are some of your hobbies?

_____

_____

_____

_____

_____

How do you feel when you're doing these hobbies?

_____

_____

_____

_____

_____

What is your dream profession? If you don't have one, what do you love to do in your spare time? Can you earn money from that activity?

_____

_____

_____

_____

_____

Does an education play a role in making this dream occupation come true?
Circle: Yes   No

How does an education play a role?

_____

_____

_____

_____

_____

Staying Motivated With a
Dream/Collage:

Because your dreams change, review these questions on the first day of each month to become more aware of your present thoughts and goals. Don't worry if your dreams and goals change. They change because you are changing. Things that were important to you five years ago are no longer important, and many things that are important to you now will not be as important to you in five years. However, one thing is for sure. *An education will play a major role in achieving each of your dreams.*

Hopefully, we're clear on the fact that an education is important in helping you achieve your goals. Let's now create an object, a Dream/Collage, to help you remember why you are studying and working so hard to obtain good grades in school.

A Dream/Collage illustrates your dreams by showing various pictures, either cut out from magazines or photographs taken of you at exciting times in your life. These pictures will be glued onto a piece of cardboard to form a collage.

Steps to creating your *Dream/Collage:*

1) Obtain old magazines and cut out pictures that bring a smile to your face. You can also collect photographs of special occasions that bring back fond memories of when you were truly blessed.
2) Paste these pictures onto a piece of cardboard large enough to hold your pictures. Feel free to make as many Dream/Collages as you desire.
3) Cut out positive quotes (that catch your eye) from various magazines and glue them onto your Dream/Collage.
4) Write your own quotes on your Dream/Collage with a magic marker.
5) Slide this cardboard Dream/Collage into a plastic cover to protect it from being damaged.
6) Put this cardboard Dream/Collage into your school binder or display it prominently in your room.
7) Review your Dream/Collage three times a day (morning, afternoon and night).

This Dream/Collage will empower your life and give you focus. When you want to give up on your history homework or you don't see why you have to pay attention in your biology class, refer to your Dream/Collage for inspiration.

If your goals are really important, you'll do whatever it takes to achieve them because you'll have focus. By becoming focused like a laser beam, you'll walk different, you'll talk different and you'll look different. You'll do your homework. You'll turn off the TV and get focused on your school work.

Without goals, I was like a source of energy, radiating but with no focus. I had no direction in my life. But with goals, my life took on new meaning. I now had a reason for studying long hours and doing well in school. With goals, my source of energy became focused. And as a result of this focus, I became empowered. This focus was so powerful that my energy became like a laser beam, powerful enough to cut through any roadblock. With this type of focus in your life, you can unlock any door to opportunity. But in order to reach your success destiny, you must know where you are going. Goals will serve this purpose for you. With goals, you will maintain focus, as you successfully move through this maze called "Life."

ROADBLOCK
1

In order to demonstrate the power of the Dream/Collage, paste a few pictures of your dreams under the following categories. Feel free to write some of your thoughts within each category as well.

FAMILY   HOUSE

FRIENDS   CAR

PROFFESSION   PHYSICAL
                                BODY

Feel free to share the seven **Dream/Collage** steps with your teachers at school. Hopefully, they will see the benefits of the Dream/Collage and wish to have all of your classmates develop their own Dream/Collage as well. Your friends and classmates will also be motivated to do their best in school so that they can move closer to achieving their goals.

With this success key, you'll definitely open many more doors of opportunity.

Congratulations! You've gotten **past the first roadblock to success known as "Suffering From Low Self-Esteem and Lacking Confidence."** You now feel better about yourself because you realize how much potential you have. You have also recognized the many things in your life which make you happy and proud. And for those things which you are not necessarily happy about, you have developed a plan for improving those particular areas of concern. You have even created your Dream/Collage. You are definitely moving closer to reaching your success destiny.

So you've gotten past this first roadblock, but how are you going to deal with that second roadblock to success known as "Failing In School"? We've talked a little about the importance of school in making your dreams come true. For me, I did not always realize this. The next chapter shares an exciting story about how I viewed school, one which you'll definitely enjoy reading.

It's 2:15, Friday afternoon. I'm in class. Turn to the next page and read how you can also overcome the second roadblock, known as "Failing In School."

Dream
Dream
Dream
Dream
Dream
Dream
Dream
Dream
Dream

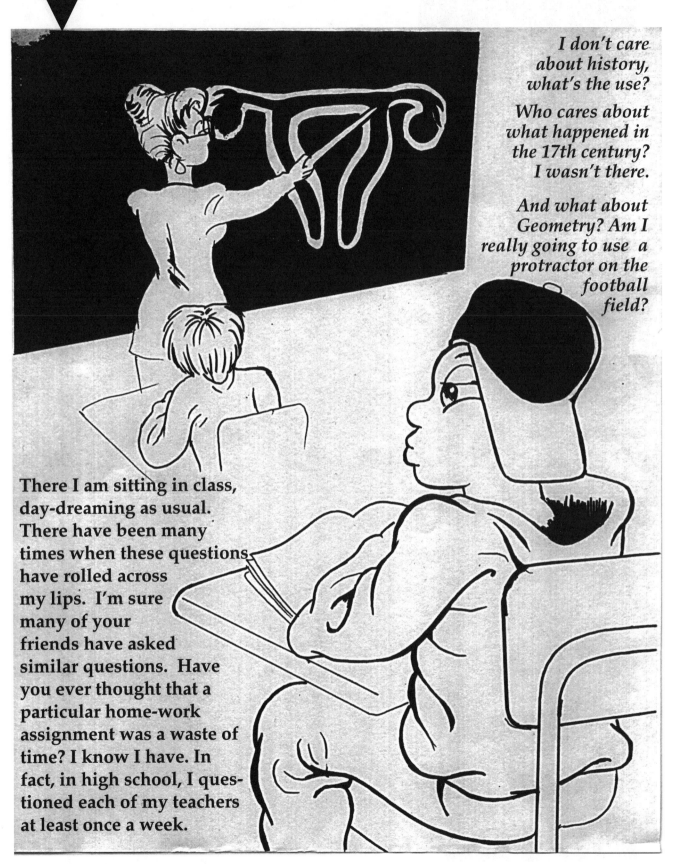

I don't care about history, what's the use?

Who cares about what happened in the 17th century? I wasn't there.

And what about Geometry? Am I really going to use a protractor on the football field?

There I am sitting in class, day-dreaming as usual. There have been many times when these questions have rolled across my lips. I'm sure many of your friends have asked similar questions. Have you ever thought that a particular home-work assignment was a waste of time? I know I have. In fact, in high school, I questioned each of my teachers at least once a week.

School Is NOT Doing Anything For Me!

I remember entering high school as a ninth grader. The most popular students were the "cool" kids. You know the ones.

They hang out in the hallways. They are always getting into trouble, by acting up in the classroom. And as a result of being the class clown, they are sent to the principal's office. And why is this? Because they're just too "cool" for school.

In my school, the most popular student was a twelfth-grader by the name of Henry Blake. He was the type of guy who was great in whatever sport he played. He was the "Michael Jordan" of our school's basketball team. He was liked by everybody. You would always see Henry strolling through the hallways with a basketball in hand and a girl by his side . He never carried any books because he was just too "cool" for school!

Although Henry was never seen studying, he did graduate. In fact, I'll never forget his senior graduation. I can see it now:

Henry is wearing sun glasses, shorts and sandals. He's just chillin'. With microphone in hand, Principal Kohkinus is calling each graduating senior to come forward to receive a high school diploma. Finally, he bellows, "Henry Blake." Henry strolls across the platform, takes his diploma, steps up to the microphone and smoothly says, "Increase the Peace!" With his "cool" walk, he just rolls across the floor. The audience goes wild, cheering for Henry.

All of my friends are in shock as we watch his "cool" walk. I'm thinking, "Henry Blake, the class clown, by far, just received the loudest applause from all the students. He is 'The Man.' I want to be just like Henry. I want to be in the in-crowd. I want to be popular like Henry."

"School is for the nerds. We don't need an education for our future careers."

During that summer vacation, my friends and I were always together playing around. We had many rap sessions. Regarding school, we reached a unanimous conclusion. The outcome was always the same: "School is for the nerds. We don't need an education for our future careers."

Chris is going to be a famous comedian. Gil aspires to become an Emmy-winning actor. Walter and I will one day be playing together in the NFL. Mark will take over the NBA with his dazzling moves, keeping everyone spellbound. Jerome will become president of his family's real estate company, becoming a millionaire in the process.

We justified our actions by saying, "We have our goals and dreams. School can't do anything for us. We don't need it for what we'll be doing. Adults just don't understand. Our parents keep hassling us about the importance of an education. They just don't understand. And let's not forget those confused teachers who are so boring. Everyday, they threaten to send us down to the principal's office if we don't stop acting up in class. What a joke!"

Coming back to school as a 10th grader after that summer vacation, I acted just like Henry: skipping classes, being the class clown, sitting in the back of the classroom, and paying no attention to my teachers. As a result, I was always being sent to the principal's office to serve detention. That's how the entire school year went.

If only I could go back to school

It did not phase me because my thoughts were, **"Hey, my grades are horrible, but that's ok, because I'm in the in-crowd."** I was very popular because I kept everyone laughing by telling jokes about the teachers. It was fun and exciting. However, one day I experienced something that shocked me. I'll never forget that day.

One day during my summer vacation prior to entering eleventh grade, my family and I went sightseeing. We went to museum after museum. It was an exhausting day. On the drive home, I had to go to the bathroom, so my dad drove into a McDonald's restaurant parking lot. I jumped out and walked briskly toward the bathroom. As I opened the bathroom door, I saw an employee mopping the floor. His back was to me. After using the bathroom, I went to the sink and turned on the faucet. While washing my hands, I said to the employee, "What's up?" The employee paused from mopping and slowly turned around. My face dropped. I was shocked. It was my idol, Henry Blake.

Henry said, "Not much is going on, just working hard." I was so stunned that I couldn't talk. I then stuttered, "School hasn't changed much." Henry said, **"That's a shame. You know when I was there, I was 'THE MAN.' And now look at me. Boy, I'll never forget the many times I was sent to Principal Kohkinus's office. He would say, 'Henry, you have so much potential but you're throwing it away...**

Your success is your choice.
It's your choice and yours only.
No one can do it for you.' "

Henry paused. A silence fell over the bathroom. Looking directly into my eyes, he said, "Nolram, at the time, I thought Kohkinus was crazy. But after graduating, I realized he was 'on it.' I should have buckled down and done my school work. When it came time to fill out an application for this job, I could hardly read the instructions. Now, I would give anything to go back to school. If I only had another chance; I would do it all different. I wouldn't skip my classes. I wouldn't be the class clown. Man, I could have had the best of both worlds: my education and the popularity. But I made the wrong choice by not valuing my education. If I could only go back and do it over. **Nolram, don't throw away your future. Look at where being cool got me."**

Suddenly the door opened and a manager, who looked much younger than Henry, walked in and snapped, "Blake, you should be finished with this floor by now! We need you to clean up a big spill in the eating area. Hurry up and get cracking!" Henry mumbled a faint "Yes, Mr. Higgins." With an embarrassed look on his face, Henry turned to me and whispered, "I gotta get back to work."

Shocked by his advice and what I had just witnessed, I had a dazed look on my face. I slowly walked toward the bathroom door with my mouth still open. This was a huge surprise. As I opened the door, I looked back over my shoulder. And there was Henry, my idol, mopping the floor. A tear was running down his cheek.

Back then, I was blind to understanding the importance of an education. I looked at myself solely as a football player and that was it. However, after seeing "cool" Henry Blake, the star basketball player, in the McDonald's bathroom, mopping floors rather than playing in the NBA, I understood, for the first time in my life, the importance of an education. I realized that my parents were right—an education is very important. I thought, "Why not become an educated football player and have the best of both worlds?"

Still stunned from the bathroom episode, I climbed back into the car. When my parents questioned my daze, I stuttered, "I....um....I....ah....need to do better.......in school." Mom and dad couldn't believe it. All along, they had been trying so hard to convince me of the importance of an education. Dad would say, "Nolram, I work hard every-day so that our family will have food on the table. All I ask of you is to get good grades in school." Mom would plead and beg me to do better in school. During parent-teacher conferences, she became sad when hearing the negative comments from my teachers. My parents talked constantly about the importance of an education. However, I wasn't listening. My response was usually, "Now look, you can't live my life. I don't need an education. I'm gonna be a football star so just get off my back, OK?"

You see, playing in the NFL was my dream. I was very talented. I had played football since the third grade and was on the right track to be picked by the pros! I started every year. I was on the first-string team playing both offense and defense each season. I received many "Most Valuable Player" awards. I was written up in the major newspapers and on some occasions, I appeared on TV. Life was exciting. I was living LARGE! From time to time, my mom said, "Nolram, this football is great and all. But you need to focus on your education. An education will pro-vide you with options." My reply was, "Come on mom, when I get that million dollar contract, I'll be set for life. And don't worry mom, I'll take care of you and dad if you're nice, ha, ha."

When my family and I finally arrived home from our sightseeing trip, I walked straight to my room and closed the door. I needed to do some serious thinking. I was still dazed from my conversation with Henry. Can you imagine? Last year's most popular student just told me that he would redo his past and change his attitude and behavior in school, **"...If only I could go back, but I can't Nolram... Don't throw away your future."** His words raced through my mind all night. I couldn't sleep. I stayed up for half the night contemplating my life and where I was heading. Fundamental questions flashed through my mind: "Were my parents right? *Henry was a great high school basketball player, but he isn't playing in the NBA.* Will the same thing happen to me and my football dreams?" Before finally drifting off to sleep, I decided to tell my close friends about this shocking experience.

Early that Sunday morning, I called my five closest friends. I asked them to come over that afternoon to watch TV and eat pizza. One by one, the "boys," Walter, Jerome, Gil, Chris and Mark entered my house. Together, we watched television. As usual, it was a fun time! However, I didn't participate in all the jokes and laughter because my mind was still focused on my conversation with Henry.

Mark asked, "What's wrong Nolram? You aren't yourself." Everybody got quiet. I asked Gil to turn off the television. He did. Taking a deep breath, I said, "The first day of school is tomorrow and I'm not sure if we're doing the right things." I proceeded to share my eye-opening conversation with Henry Blake. There was complete silence in the room.

I ended by saying, "Are we throwing away our future by acting the fool and being class clowns in school?"

Don't throw away your future.

> After a few moments of silence, I fell victim to the peer pressure from my friends.
>
> I slowly replied, "Yeah, I guess you're right."

KA-BOOOOOOM!
Walter jumped up and shouted, "I'm a football player and so are you. Wake up man, school is for fools."

"When we make the pros, we'll be getting paid IN FULL. Think about the multi-million dollar contracts. That's what we'll be receiving while those nerds will be barely making it, living from paycheck to paycheck. I'm gonna get paid in full. And ain't no chemistry or foreign language class gonna get me there."

Gil added, "Yeah, that's right. Sylvester Stallone doesn't have a college degree and look how well he's done with his acting career. Rocky is known around the world. Do you really think the movie producers asked what his S.A.T. scores were? NOT, I don't think so."

After a few moments of silence, I fell victim to the peer pressure from my friends. I slowly replied, "Yeah, I guess you're right. I've already got some college football scouts looking at me with the intention of giving me a football scholarship." Walter turned the TV back on. And we continued to joke as we watched television and ate more pizza. That afternoon turned out to be another great time with "the boys."

First Day Of School

Early that next morning, my mom shouted, "Nolram, wake up! It's time for school." Still half-dazed, I replied, "I'm up," then fell right back to sleep. Ten minutes later, she screamed, "Nolram, are you up? School will be starting in one hour. You don't want to be late to your first day of school." Being spaced-out, I said, "Yeah, yeah, yeah," but still didn't move. Having her first two attempts fail, mom came into my room and shouted in a commanding voice, "Get up" as she pulled off the blankets. Ice-cold air ran up my legs and revitalized me into consciousness as I jumped straight up. "Now come on, Nolram. Get up!" she yelled. She was serious.

I stumbled into the bathroom, bumping into the desk and walls along the way. My body wasn't used to getting up so early. The first day of school was always the hardest. Getting used to waking up early was a real challenge for me, like for so many of us. After screaming as the ice-cold water made contact with my shivering body in the shower, I was finally up. "It's my own fault," I thought. "Just my luck, there's no more hot water because everyone else has already taken a long hot shower. As usual, I am the last one."

That morning, mom fixed breakfast. As I sat down at the kitchen table, she asked, "So you're going to do better in school?" In order to please her, I responded, "Yeah, sure." But after my conversation with "the boys" yesterday, I knew full-well that I was a football player and didn't need an education. Although Henry had jolted me with his shocking advice, I rationalized by thinking, "I'm an outstanding football player and I'm gonna make it."

The only reason that I went to school was to see my friends and play football.

The Football Season

This school year started out just like the other school years. My close friends and I did our usual routine of strolling into class late, sitting in the back, acting up and being disruptive to the teacher. Our daily routine was typical. We just played at school, cut jokes on the students who did their homework, went to football practice, hung out at the mall, and talked for countless hours on the phone. The only reason that I went to school was to see my friends and play football.

The football team was great. Walter and I made unbelievable plays on the football field. We were both selected as team captains. Neither one of us could wait until the school day was over so we could begin our football practice. Everything was going smooth until that first game.

One of the most unbelievable events in my life occurred during that first game of the season. It was a dreary, raining day. The sun was hidden by the clouds. The rain, sinking into the ground, made the field very slippery.

It was fourth quarter, three minutes left in the game. Our team was winning 14 to 13. The other team had the ball and was moving down the field. Walter screamed, "They're on our thirty yard line. Boom, another first down. Now they're on our eighteen yard line."

We huddled up and I shouted, "Come on now. It's on us. We've got to stop them." We broke our defensive huddle with the usual, "One, Two, Three, BREAK!"

The Football Season

Our defensive team lined up. Now, there was a minute and thirteen seconds remaining in the game. The other team broke from their huddle and lined up. The quarterback slowly approached his position. To break his concentration, I looked the quarterback directly in the eyes and started growling, "GRRRRRR, You are mine." I was pumped up.

The quarterback shouted, "Hut 1, Hut 2, Hike!" And then everything went into slow motion. With football in hand, the quarterback dropped back into the backfield. I started back-peddling as fast as I could because it was going to be a pass. The quarterback threw a short pass to his receiver down field. The receiver caught the ball and got by one of my teammates. I was hot on the pursuit, running as fast as I could to tackle the receiver.

And here it was, the receiver and me. It was him against me, one on one. I had to stop him. As I went to tackle him, my feet came out from underneath me as I slipped on the wet grass. While falling, in desperation, I threw out my arm to trip the receiver.

SNAP!!!- AHHHHHHHHHHH!

Pain shot up and down my arm. I screamed as I fell onto the ground. The pain hurt so much. As I rolled on the ground, screaming at the top of my lungs, my coaches ran onto the field. I had no control over my arm. My first thought was, "I broke my arm." It hung down to the ground. I couldn't move it. I had no control over my arm.

There I lay on the field in pain crying like a new-born baby.

The coaches tried to calm me down by saying, "It's going to be OK." But they didn't feel my pain. I shouted, "It hurts, help me!" Coach Johnson said, "Nolram, stay still. Don't move." I continued screaming, "IT HURTS. Help me, I'm in PAIN!"

When the coach touched my arm, I shouted. It felt like I was being stabbed with a butcher knife. There I lay helpless on the field.

I overheard one coach say, "This is bad, get the ambulance out here."

The Football Season

As I lay there, totally helpless, I thought to myself, "I can't believe this. I never thought I would get hurt. I'm usually the one dishing out the pain and now here I am, helpless, in total pain." The pain had grown worse.

I just wanted this to be a bad dream. It seemed as though time froze. Seconds seemed like minutes. Minutes became hours as I continued to scream in pain!

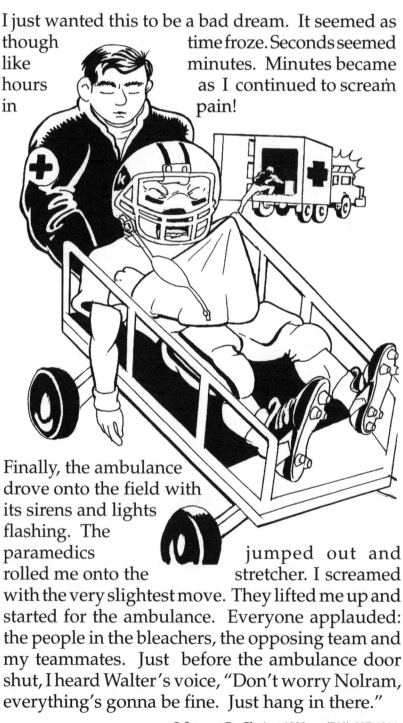

I couldn't believe it. I was hurt, real bad.

Finally, the ambulance drove onto the field with its sirens and lights flashing. The paramedics jumped out and rolled me onto the stretcher. I screamed with the very slightest move. They lifted me up and started for the ambulance. Everyone applauded: the people in the bleachers, the opposing team and my teammates. Just before the ambulance door shut, I heard Walter's voice, "Don't worry Nolram, everything's gonna be fine. Just hang in there."

The Football Season

The ambulance quickly drove away with sirens screaming and lights twirling. As I lay on the stretcher, I felt helpless. I thought about my NFL dreams. My mind played the all-to-familiar voice of mom saying,"*An education will provide you with options, Nolram. An education will open up doors.*"

Finally, the ambulance pulled up to the emergency entrance of the hospital. Hours went by at the hospital. Many X-rays were taken. The nurses gave me pain killers. But this medication didn't help relieve the pain. Pain shot up and down my arm with the slightest move. Because I was hurting, I continually hassled the nurses to bring the doctor. And finally, the doctor walked into my room and said, "Son, I've got some good news and some bad news. Which do you care to hear first?"

Confusion and fear filled my mind. I nervously stuttered, "The bad news first." Walking towards me, the doctor said, "Son, your arm is out of socket. It's dislocated." I screamed, "NO, not me!" I couldn't believe it. My arm is out of socket. No, no, no, not me. I'm Nolram, the professional football player. This must be a bad nightmare. What could possibly be the good news? With sincerity in his voice, the doctor responded, "The good news is ....I'm going to put it back into socket now." As tears rolled down my cheek, the doctor took my arm and said, "Son, this might hurt."And with one fierce yank, my shoulder was back in place. It was now in socket.

An education will provide you with options, Nolram.

An education will open up doors.

I thought, "I can't believe this. I'm out for the season. What about the NFL? Wow, what am I going to do now."

While driving home from the hospital with my mom, numerous thoughts bombarded my mind:

Henry Blake saying, "If only I could go back to school. Don't throw your education away."

My parents saying how an education will provide options in today's competitive society.

My friends saying that school is for nerds. "We don't need it!"

I was totally confused about my future and how I would deal with this situation.

Help Me! What should I do?

Feeling helpless in a sling and not able to play football, I had to consider some other possibilities. Maybe Henry and my parents were right about the importance of an education. Maybe I should try to do better in school. I thought, "Wow, I'll have to change my attitude and behavior in order to learn in school. Right now, my grades are horrible. Can I really turn it around?"

Now I Know Why
School is Important

The next day at school, friends came up to me and said how sorry they were for me. With my shoulder in a sling, I cautiously strolled to class early to avoid being bumped in the hallway. I sat up in the front of each class and paid close attention while my close friends, Walter and ⌐ ⌐ crew, sat in the back, disrupting the class by cutting up.

My transformation had begun. For the next two weeks, I came to class on time and participated in the lessons by asking questions of the teacher. I completed my homework and turned it in on time. And as a result, my grades improved dramatically. I began to understand the importance of an education.

By participating in classroom discussions and working on challenging homework assignments, I realized that I was not stupid. It was a great feeling to know that I could do it. I felt proud when I correctly answered the teacher's questions. The same feeling that I had experienced on the football field was now taking place in the classroom. I was "on it," taking care of business. In regard to my education, I was now scoring touchdowns in the classroom. My grades improved in all of my classes.

One day, after finishing my lunch, I went to throw away my trash. As I dropped my cup in the trash can, someone said, "Hey, teacher's pet, goodie-two-shoes." I slowly turned around and to my surprise, my four closest friends were approaching me with serious looks on their faces.

Upset, Walter asked, "What's up Nolram? Ever since your injury, you haven't been the same. You don't hang out with us anymore at the mall. You tell us that you have to get off the phone so you can do your homework. You don't even sit with us anymore in the back of the classroom. You've changed."

Peer Pressure Is Crazy!

Peer Pressure Is Crazy!

Shocked, I nervously replied, "Man, Walter, you brothers are my best friends. We've all been real tight since kindergarten. I'm down. But I'm also trying to better myself. Remember what happened to Henry Blake? We all need to do better in school so that we will have options and choices after graduating from ......"

Cutting me off and jumping in my face, Gil moved closer and shouted, "Look Nolram, don't give us that noise. You're starting to sound like our parents. You're like a broken record saying the same thing over and over."

Chris demanded, "Nolram, either you're down with us or you're not. It's that simple. Either you're part of the crew or you stand alone. What's it gonna be?"

Many conflicting thoughts bombarded my mind simultaneously...

Walter interrupted my thoughts by asking, "What's it gonna be?" With tears welling up in my eyes, I responded, "Why can't we do well in school and hang tight after our studies are done?" No one budged, conveying that I had to make a choice.

How would you handle this situation if you were I?

The great memories, many laughs, and good times with "the boys."

My conversation with Henry Blake.

The sense of accomplishment I experienced when I received a high test score.

Peer Pressure Is Crazy!

That moment illustrated a success principle:

You must stand for something or you'll fall for anything. An education provides options.

Stand up for your education!

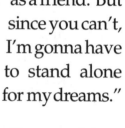

I couldn't believe it. Here were my life-long friends challenging me. I'm either part of the group or I'm left out. After a long, deep breath, I finally replied, "Friends encourage friends to be their best. I wish you would respect my decision to do better in school as a friend. But since you can't, I'm gonna have to stand alone for my dreams."

Everything went into slow motion. To this day, I have never forgotten my friends turning their backs on me and walking down the hallway. My best friends were gone. I stood alone. I started questioning my decision. "Are you crazy, Nolram? That was stupid." Although it hurt, I knew that I was doing the right thing even though it wasn't the popular thing. An education will give me more opportunities. I stood my ground. That day, my closest friends walked away from me and our friendship fell apart. It was one of the most difficult decisions of my life.

Although my decision was painful, I began to understand the power of following my heart rather than following the crowd. As a future leader, realize that your decisions to stand for what you believe in will sometimes be challenged.

Peer Pressure Is Crazy!

In fact, many students across this nation put down and make fun of other students who try to excel in their academic studies. The March 16, 1992, edition of <u>Time</u> magazine includes an article titled "The Hidden Hurdle." The pain of striving for academic excellence is illustrated by the following excerpt:

When it comes to achieving in school, Za'kettha Blaylock knows that even dreaming of success can mean living a nightmare. She would, above all things, like to work hard, go to college and become a doctor. But to many other black 14-year-old girls in her corner of Oakland, these ideas are anathema. The telephone rings in her family's modest apartment, and the anonymous voice murmurs daggers. "We're gonna kill you," the caller says. Za'kettha knows the threat comes from a gang of black girls, one that specializes not in drugs or street fights but in terrorizing bright black students. "They think that just because you're smart," says the eighth-grader, "they can go around beating you up." Of all the obstacles to success that students face, the most surprising and discouraging may be those erected by their own peers.

...."They'll run up to you and grab your books and say, 'I'll tear this book up,' " says Shaquila Williams, 12, a sixth-grader at Webster Academy in East Oakland. "They'll try and stop you from doing your work." Honor students may be rebuked for even showing up for class on time. This pattern of abuse is a distinctive variation of the nerd bashing that almost all bright, ambitious students— no matter what their color — face at some point in their lives.

In my school, I remember how the hardest-working students were often teased for turning in their homework or answering questions in class.

Are you a hard-working student or are you the one who tries to pull others down?

Circle your answer:

class-clown **\<or\>** committed student!

Realize this, you must stand for something or you'll fall for anything.

An EDUCATION Opens Doors!

Peer Pressure Is Crazy!

It is true: **An education opens up doors!** Ask yourself, "Do I plan to fail?" I'll bet your reply is "No." Most of your friends don't plan to fail, either. Of course, everyone wishes to be rich, happy and successful. That's easy! But the real question is, "Are you failing to plan?" It takes more energy to think about your future and plan your success. An education will definitely play a major role in that plan.

Unfortunately, many students are drifting through school from one class to the next without completing their homework or answering the teacher's questions within the classroom. They are not gaining as much knowledge as they could from their classes. Although many say they don't plan to fail, their actions are speaking so loud that we no longer listen to their words. Due to their actions, they are walking on a path to a future with limited options because they chose the wrong door in regard to an "Education" in this maze called "Life." If they had only chosen the door where they applied themselves in school and obtained good grades, more doors would open up later in life. But unfortunately, like Henry Blake, they chose to walk through the door marked "School is NOT Important," and now they're paying the price. Hopefully, you'll learn from Henry's mistake and strive to do your best in school. Please hold on to your focus and don't let the distractions get you off course when it comes to doing well in school.

The reason I share this with you is because it wasn't long ago that I was in your same position. Prior to my conversation with Henry Blake and dislocating my shoulder, I didn't value an education. I didn't see its importance. But I have now realized the value of an education. Hopefully, you have learned a lesson from reading both Henry's and my story.

What are your plans after completing high school?

_____

_____

_____

Do you enjoy school? Circle: Yes   No

What do you like about school?

_____

_____

_____

What do you dislike about school?

_____

_____

_____

What can you do to improve the things that you don't like about school?

_____

_____

_____

Which classes do you like and why?

_____

_____

_____

Who are some of your role models?

_____

_____

_____

How many of your role models have a high school diploma? _____
How many of your role models have a college degree? _____

How Can I Make Big Money?

"More money, more money, more money," my friend Jason whispers to me.

He continues with, "I'm gonna get paid in full! I'll be living large. Picture this: me flying all over the world, going into any high-priced department store and buying anything that catches my eye without even looking at the price tag. That's me, living the good life."

I listen and wisely ask ,"How are you going to earn all this money?"

Shocked, Jason, the dreamer, stutters, "I don't know."

Isn't that the case for most of us? As young people, we day-dream about how our lives will be when we're older. Close your eyes right now and picture how your life will be in thirty years.

What will you be doing? Answer here.

_____
_____
_____

Now, close your eyes again and tell me what you will be doing in ten years. In a few sentences, write down what you will be doing in ten years to make your thirty-year dreams come true.

_____
_____
_____

Great, that's wonderful. Now in order for your dreams to come true, describe what you have to achieve by next year. Take three minutes to concentrate and focus on how you will be living your life. Write down what you'll achieve by next year in order to make your future dreams come true.

_____
_____
_____
_____
_____

How Can I Make Big Money?

During one summer job, I asked Mr. Thomas, my manager, "How important are grades in this company's hiring process?" Mr. Thomas replied, "They play a critical role. For example, Nolram, one time we had more than 1,000 applicants competing for three job openings." I shouted, "Wow, it must have taken you a long time to review all those applications!" Mr. Thomas replied, "No, we just separated their applications by GPA(Grade Point Average). I went through each of the 1,000 applications looking only at GPAs. And based on GPAs, I put the applications in three different piles. One pile was for students who had a GPA under 2.0. Another pile consisted of students in the GPA range of a 2.1 to 3.0. The third pile consisted of those students with GPAs of 3.1 to 4.0. Nolram, when I had finished, I discovered that I had approximately 400 applications in the 3.1 to 4.0 GPA group. I then discarded the other 600 applications without even looking past their GPAs. For the 400 applications still remaining, I separated them into two groups: those students with a GPA greater than a 3.5 and those with a GPA less than a 3.5. There turned out to be some 125 applications in the 3.5-4.0 GPA range. I discarded the other 275 applications and read only the 125 applications to fill the three open positions."

Stand up right now and go in front of the mirror. Look into your eyes, and answer this question: **"How am I going to make my dreams come true?"**

This is a serious question that takes much thought. Don't worry if you haven't decided yet because you'll be OK as long as you continue doing your best in school by obtaining excellent grades. I know this to be true because I've been there.

An education plays a major role in making your dreams come true.

GRADES MATTER
A
B
C
D
F

Good Grades:
A Key To Happiness

The indisputable fact is that an education provides opportunity. An education is similar to a key which opens up many doors. Although you may have a door key, it might be the wrong key for that particular door. Bad grades represent the wrong key to the door of opportunity. It's not enough to just barely get by and receive a high school diploma. Good grades and letters of recommendation from teachers represent a master key which opens up many more doors to an unlimited possibility of professions and careers. And being in this maze called "Life," you will want to obtain the master key that opens many locked doors, so that you're able to continue your journey of success. An education will definitely play a role in the success that you achieve.

Most students across this nation want to be successful and happy. After obtaining their high school diplomas, most students plan to continue their success by either going to college and/or obtaining a high-paying job. But how will they achieve this?

Grades matter! Grades can be the ultimate factor in whether you are offered admission to the college of your dreams. There are many great athletes who lost their college scholarships because of their grades or S.A.T. scores. Companies across this world are becoming lean-mean-fighting-machines. They are looking to hire talented young people. Many companies use grades as an indication of a student's potential. In some instances, a new employee's salary could be based on his or her overall GPA as well as in which particular classes he or she achieved academic excellence. Let's be serious. To receive an "A" in gym does not carry the same impression as receiving an "A" in calculus. Grades do indeed matter, but so do your classes. Do your best in school because you deserve an exciting future with many options.

An Education Opens Doors!

Understand this, you and I are playing in the game of life. Just as Michael Jordan played by certain guidelines in the game of basketball, most celebrity entertainers commit to perfecting their skills by practicing eight to twelve hours a day. And that's true commitment.

Although you and I may not desire to become a superstar athlete or entertainer, we are still playing by certain guidelines in the game of life. And to succeed in achieving our personal goals, we must make the commitment to our education. There are no free rides.

Let's not forget, even Michael Jordan took the S.A.T. examination and went to college in order to pursue his dream of playing professional basketball.

It's competitive out here. Yet some of us are failing to plan ahead. But it's not too late for you. You have a choice!

Repeat this aloud:

*"If it's to be,
then it's up to me."*

*Stand up! Go to the mirror
and look into your eyes
and shout, "If it's to be,
then it's up to me!"*

*It's your choice
and yours only.*

You see, in this game of life, here are the facts:

- **High school dropouts earn one-third that of high school graduates.**

- **84 percent of prison inmates are high school dropouts.**

- **High school dropouts are three times more likely to be unemployed compared to high school graduates.**

"My Past Does Not Dictate My Future"

Your Past Does Not Dictate Your Future

Remember the story of Henry Blake, the great high school basketball player who was mopping bathroom floors? Due to his bad grades, he didn't have any other options. He failed to plan. And what about me, who used to be a class clown? I didn't have the greatest grades either. My focus was on my football career. However, after my devastating injury and being in a sling for eight weeks, I had time to think about my future and where I was headed. By changing my priorities from hanging out with friends and acting-the-fool, to applying myself in school, my focus shifted to improving my grades. No more lip service. Results are what count! I changed my actions and worked hard in school. And as a result, my grades improved.

Your past does not dictate your future. Repeat this statement out loud, "My past does not dictate my future." You can't change your past, but you do control your future. In the quarter before my football injury, I had a 1.6 GPA, a "D" average. That next quarter, I worked and studied long hours and achieved a 2.8 GPA, a "B-" average. The third quarter, when I realized that studying pays off, I continued the momentum as I obtained a 3.4 GPA, a "B+" average. Then I worked hard, and I mean *HARD*. By concentrating and focusing my attention on my classes, I achieved my goal. I got all "A's" on my report card during the fourth quarter.

You see, grades do not tell how smart you are but rather how disciplined you are. Everyone reading this book can be on the honor roll. Yes, that means you, too. Now, some things do come easier to some students. But hey, I had a 1.6 GPA, and a few quarters later, all "A's." What made the difference? Did my brain get larger and smarter? Absolutely not! I just changed my habits and became "too legit to quit" because I wanted options in my life. I realized that an education would give me options. And for you, an education will give you options as well. Don't mess up your opportunity to do your best in school and obtain great grades. It would be a shame if you ended up like basketball star Henry Blake, wishing you could return to school and do things right.

Too Legit To Quit

At this very moment, colleges and companies are looking at your track record. They want to see an improvement in your grades, an upward progression. They take into consideration the adjustments you might have to make when entering a new school with new teachers and new classes. However, colleges and companies believe that once a student gets focused and accustomed to this new environment, a committed student will obtain better grades. Are your grades improving? Maybe they have, maybe they have not.

Forget about what your grades were last year, or last report card or even last week! The past is in the past. You can't change it. You can only learn from it and move on! Now focus on preparing for next week's test, tomorrow's quiz or tonight's homework assignment. Do it now. Remember, most students do not plan to fail in life. However, many fail to plan. Take responsibility for your life and do your best in school.

Excelling in school creates options. I'm not talking about just getting by. But rather, doing your best in school. It will foster a sense of pride. Knowing your stuff allows you to walk with confidence. You'll develop a winning mindset: a mindset of **"Being Too Legit - Too Legit To Quit."**

"Too legit to quit" means going the extra yard. As you know, playing football was my main goal in life. However, after I separated my shoulder, I had two operations. While recuperating from the surgeries, I couldn't play any sports in the eleventh grade. This was a sad time in my life as I watched Walter and other players work together to win games without me. However, it also turned out to be a blessed time as I discovered how much school has to offer.

By working on challenging problems, I began to learn how to become a true thinker. School became fun as I correctly answered tough questions.

Life was great during that semester.

I was on the honor roll by obtaining all "A's" and "B's" on my report card. And at the same time, I was nominated MVP of the entire football league. I had the best of both worlds. It can be done. If you so desire, you, too, can be an educated athlete.

An Educated Athlete – More Money

When my teachers returned corrected tests , I felt proud to see a high test score or grade. Excitement ran through my body when I answered a difficult question correctly. Because of my new commitment to my studies, my grades were at an all-time high. But still lingering in my mind was the dream of playing football once again. I had to do it. It was part of me. After weightlifting and running every day to rebuild my body, I was ready to go after my starting postion on the football team. I felt great. I had the best of both worlds, excelling in school with high test scores while preparing to rejoin the football team.

During my senior year, I came back to play football. At that first practice, my coaches told me that they were glad to see me back. However, since I had missed one full year of playing football, they said that I must fight to earn my starting position back. The coaches placed me at fourth string. However, being "too legit to quit," I was committed to giving my best. With persistence and hard work, I moved up from fourth string to reclaim my starting position before the first game of the season. I was on a mission to do my best.

That year, I was blessed with a great season. I was mentioned on the local NBC affiliate's "Sports Machine" for having many outstanding games. I was placed on the All-Division football team. And, as the ultimate reward, I caught the winning touchdown pass in the Class 'A' State Championship game.

The football season was great. I played the best games of my life. But even more exciting was the fact that I had excelled in the classroom as well by obtaining high test scores. I realized that mom and dad were right: An education provides true opportunity. A good education represents a master key in this maze called "Life." And because I wanted to receive my master key, I focused my attention on doing extremely well in school. By holding the master key, I could open up many doors to various opportunities. An education truly gives us more options.

An Educated Athlete -More Money

*An education
will help you achieve
your dreams.*

Are you happy with your grades? Please explain.

_____
_____
_____

Is it important to improve your grades? Please explain.

_____
_____
_____

How will your education help you accomplish your goals?

_____
_____

List ways in which you can improve your grades.

_____
_____
_____

What will you do right now to improve your grades?

_____
_____
_____

The Michael Jordan Showdown

Where would Michael Jordan be if he had always been the class clown who never did his homework, did poorly on the SAT examination, and was always being sent down to the principal's office for detention?

The college basketball scholarship to play for the North Carolina Tar Heels would never have been offered. And if he had not played college basketball, the Chicago Bulls would not have selected Michael Jordan in the basketball draft.

No matter what your goal or dream profession is, you have to be a thinker in order to excel. On the basketball court, Michael Jordan had to make split-second decisions that required him to be a thinker of the truest meaning.

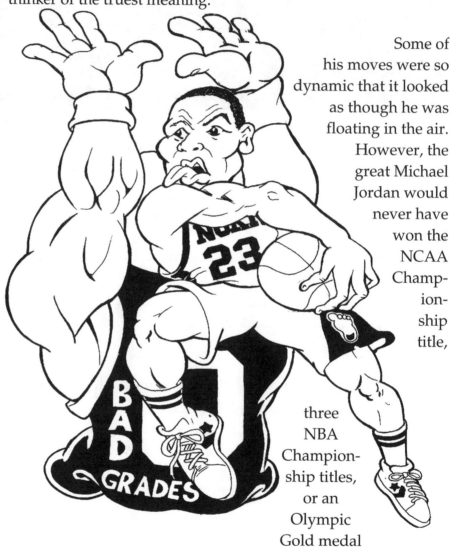

Some of his moves were so dynamic that it looked as though he was floating in the air. However, the great Michael Jordan would never have won the NCAA Championship title, three NBA Championship titles, or an Olympic Gold medal if he had not gone to college. In fact, it is highly unlikely that Michael Jordan would have played for the Chicago Bulls if he had not done well in school or scored well enough on the SAT to enter college. Michael Jordan is a thinker. He took world history, chemistry, algebra and a foreign language while playing high school basketball. If he had not done well in school, the door to a fantastic basketball career never would have opened. Bad grades would have prevented Michael Jordan from playing in the NBA. Can you imagine the NBA without Michael Jordan? Neither can I.

The Michael Jordan Showdown

Are you a student-athlete?
If you are,
or have friends who are,
tell everyone that grades
are now the law of the land!

The NCAA passed Proposition 42, which denies any scholarships to athletes who fail to meet basic requirements, essentially:

1) **A "C" average in 11 high school core classes, and**
2) **A score of 700 (on a scale of 400 to 1,600) on the SAT**

   or 15 (on a scale of 1 to 36) on the ACT.

In fact, the NCAA is considering raising these academic standards even to a higher level. This is no joke. In order to demonstrate your dynamic moves on the playing field, you have to score the high marks in the classroom as well. It would be a shame if your grades held you back from becoming a professional superstar.

ROADBLOCK
2

It's Never Too Late

So now you realize the importance of an education.

But you're saying to yourself "It's too late, I'm flunking all my classes. My grades are terrible."

Never forget this statement: "The past does not dictate the future." No matter what your grades were last year, last semester, or even yesterday, that does not matter now. Today is a new day and that is where your focus should be. We can't change the past, the past is gone. All we can do is learn from the past and move on. So don't worry if your grades are not as good as they could be, not all is lost.

One semester I received a depressing 1.6 GPA. Yes, a 1.6 GPA (a "D" average)! But that wasn't the end of my future. Rather than blame my teachers, I assumed personal responsibility for my grades. I moved up to a 2.8 (a "B-" average) and then to a 3.4 (a "B+" average), and finally, all "A's." Now, I don't share this with you to impress you, but rather to impress upon you the fact that you can do anything you want if you're committed to do what it takes to achieve your goal. My mind didn't become smarter over the course of a few semesters. No, no, no, rather, my actions changed allowing me to succeed in school and improve my grades. Although I love to party, hang out at the mall, talk on the phone, and watch TV, I realized that I had to reduce the amount of time I was spending on these activities and focus my attention on my studies and homework. I needed to have balance: play hard and work hard.

Listen to me, grades do not tell how smart you are. I repeat, **grades do not tell how smart you are.** Rather, grades tell how disciplined you are and show your commitment. All children have the ability to learn. Now it is true that some children pick up things a little faster than others. But that doesn't matter. Each one of us has been blessed with a brain. And what's important is how you use your brain. Remember, your brain is the greatest computer on the face of this earth.

© Success By Choice, 1993 • (510) 887-1311

It's Never Too Late

Consider me as an example! The only thing that changed and allowed me to go from a 1.6 GPA to all "A's" is the fact that I changed my study habits. After reading this next section, you will discover tips for improving your grades as well.

What were your grades on your last report card?
_____
_____
_____

Are you happy and proud of these grades? Please explain.
_____
_____
_____

Do you have a balanced life? Do you play hard and work hard? Please explain.
_____
_____
_____

How can you improve your grades?
_____
_____
_____

Wonderful, you now realize the importance of school. But how will you improve your grades? That's the real question. Let's now overcome this possible roadblock of "Failing in School" by obtaining success keys for "Succeeding in School." With these success keys in your hand, you will open many doors of opportunity. Turn the page and read how you can use these keys in your life and learn more while improving your grades. It's 6:15, Friday evening. I'm doing my homework.

Success Keys For Succeeding In School

I'm in my room doing my homework. I've spent forty-five minutes on the first problem. I'm frustrated and need help. My mom walks into my room and asks, "How's it going, Nolram?"

Frustrated, I respond, "Darn it, mom, this homework is too difficult. Last night, I spent three hours on one homework problem and still got it wrong. I'm trying so hard but it's not paying off. I just want to give up!"

My mom tries to comfort me but it doesn't help. I'm still upset.

Don't Do It By Yourself

Have you ever experienced this? Most students have encountered this at one time or another. What do you think are some possible solutions?

_____

_____

_____

How do you study? What is your technique for learning a new class lesson.

_____

_____

_____

Do you get help when needed? If so, what is your method for getting help? If not, answer why not.

_____

_____

_____

I think one solution is working smarter rather than working harder.

Success Keys for Succeeding In School

The following four suggestions will help you work smarter and reap the benefits from your effort. Use all four suggestions and your grades will improve. My grades went from a 1.6 GPA to all "A's" by utilizing these four suggestions. Implement these suggestions in your life and watch your grades improve.

Academic Excellence Tip #1:
TEACHERS

Outside of each class period, make a commitment to see at least one teacher each day of every week. During your time with them, obtain answers to questions that you have regarding a particular homework assignment or test. For example, if you have five different teachers, you could arrange your schedule to see one particular teacher every Monday, another teacher every Tuesday, and so on through Friday. You may choose to visit your teachers before school, during lunch or after school. Each day can be reserved for a particular teacher. At this moment, write in the provided spaces which teacher(s) you will visit each day of this upcoming week.

Monday _____   Thursday _____
Tuesday _____   Friday   _____
Wednesday _____

By spending time outside of class with your teachers, they will recognize your commitment to your education. They will become more willing to spend extra time with you because of your commitment to academic excellence. If a teacher believes you are working extremely hard to learn the class material, that teacher will be more willing to help you succeed. In addition, many teachers will possibly write letters of recommendation for you. This will benefit you when seeking college admission or employment.

Success Keys for Succeeding In School

Academic Excellence Tip #2: Tutors

If tutors are available, utilize them. After each test or homework assignment is corrected and returned, have the tutor and/or teacher explain the correct answers to the questions that were marked incorrect. This is critical to your success. In many subjects, the course material builds upon previously-taught material. Therefore, it is critical for you to keep up with the material of each class and not let it become overwhelming. Do not let it become like an avalanche crashing on your head at the end of the quarter or semester. On a regular basis, meet with your tutors as much as possible.

Success Keys for Succeeding In School

Academic Excellence Tip #3:
STUDY GROUPS

My grades improved tremendously once I started studying with certain friends. This is an excellent suggestion to help boost your understanding of the studies as well as to enjoy the studying process. Select three to six classmates to study with for a certain number of days per week. Write their names here:

1. _____
2. _____
3. _____
4. _____
5. _____
6. _____

Each session will last for a few hours. For example, it could be two hours each night, Monday through Friday.

Or maybe, it will be four hours on Saturday and Sunday and three hours on Wednesday. This will be the decision of the group. However, once the decision is made, each member must commit to attending each session. What days will your study group get together?

_____

_____

It is important that each student participating in the study group be supportive of the other study group members. The purpose of the study group is for students to come together and help one another understand the course material. This could mean doing homework assignments together. And just as well, your group could study together for upcoming quizzes and tests. By working together, everyone will prosper.

Success Keys for Succeeding In School

Academic Excellence Tip #3:
STUDY GROUPS

Each study group member must adhere to the rules and guidelines set by the group. The most important guideline is that the group will study for forty-five minutes followed by a fifteen minute break. A time keeper must be selected by the group members. The time keeper must maintain order by starting both the study period and break on time.

Realize this: when friends come together, there is a possibility that the session will get out of control. Chit-chat, gossiping and fun could possibly take over the study session. Time slots could even reverse where studying occurs for only fifteen minutes followed by forty-five minutes of play. The study group must stay focused. Keep the study group's main goal in mind, which is to help you and your friends learn and improve your grades. Rather than studying alone and getting stuck, it is helpful to study with a group and get help when needed. However, the group must focus on the mission of the study group, which is for each member to obtain a better understanding of the class lesson. This will result in better grades for all members of your group. Decide on a name for your study group.

What will be the name of your study group?

| |
| |

Academic Excellence Tip #4:
PARENTS/MENTORS

Another suggestion is to have your parent(s) and mentor(s) become involved in your study group. They have much knowledge and will take pride in seeing your study group become successful! In addition to getting them involved, you may want to share your studies with them every night. Keep them informed of what you're learning in school. Ask for examples of how your daily school lesson is applied in the REAL world. Ask them for examples so you can understand how your school lesson is used in the REAL world.

How will these four suggestions help you improve your grades?

_____
_____
_____
_____

When will you utilize these four suggestions?

_____
_____
_____
_____

Are there any other strategies that you will use to improve your grades.

_____
_____
_____
_____

With these success keys in your pocket, you will definitely open more doors of opportunity. Before you begin reading the next chapter, let me ask you this question: *"How important is an education to you?"* **Please explain.**

_____
_____
_____
_____

HOOORAH · HOOORAH

**Success Keys for
Succeeding In School**

An education
will give you knowledge
and help develop
your skills
to their fullest potential.

Today, a quality education
is no longer a choice.
It is a MUST!

*Hooooorah,
I've
graduated
from
high school.*

Because you have read
this chapter,
you now have
the success keys
for succeeding in school.
You and I are both on our journey
to success and everlasting happiness.

I'm now off to college...

It's 2:30, Sunday afternoon, and I've just been dropped off at college.
I'm all alone. I'm scared.
Turn the page and read the next chapter
and check out my college experience.

With tears flowing down my face, I watched my parents drive off down the road. I waved good-bye. Part of me wanted them to make a U-turn and take me back home. The other part of me was happy to see them go because I was now on my own. I was finally in college.

As my parent's car disappeared out of sight, I slowly turned to walk up to my new home—the freshman dormitory. Many thoughts raced through my mind:

"Am I smart enough to succeed here?"
"Will I one day graduate or will I fail out?"
"Will I be accepted here?"
"None of my high school friends are here, can I make new friends?"

There were countless questions on my mind. It was just a matter of time until I would find out the answers.

What questions do you have regarding your college experience?

_____

_____

_____

_____

_____

I'll never forget when my roommate first walked into our dormitory room. There was complete silence! Seconds seemed like countless minutes. He finally broke the silent showdown by hesitantly saying, "I'm Bill." I replied, "Hi, my name is Nolram."

We were both nervous. He was a stranger to me. And I was a stranger to him. However, as we helped one another unpack our boxes and decorate the room, we became more comfortable. We let down our guards and began to joke with one another. Hours flew by! And before we knew it, it was 1:30 in the morning. We were exhausted. We had a trying day due to all the unpacking of boxes after the long car ride to school. So we prepared to go to sleep by brushing our teeth and changing into our pajamas. We turned off the lights and told one another good night.

In complete darkness, as I lay in bed, I thought about how much I missed my high school friends. I was somewhat nervous but yet excited about my first year at college.

My First Year At College

And what an exciting year it was. There were many parties, all-night study sessions, beautiful girls, outstanding sporting events, encouraging professor and challenging classes.

Unfortunately, some of my close friends who started college with me did not finish. After that first semester, they were gone. They dropped out for one reason or another. The reasons ranged from receiving bad grades to obtaining no financial support to lacking focus in their studies to not handling the freedom of college.

It was very sad because I am no smarter than they. And yet, I was able to graduate from college with an electrical engineering degree. The only reason I made it was because I kept my priorities in check.

> **Whatever your goals may be, whether you succeed or fail to reach your goals depends on one person and ONE person only— YOU!**

Answer this question, "Why do you want to go to college?"

_____

_____

_____

_____

Is it because of your parents? Is it to get excellent grades? Is it to get a great job? Or maybe you're just following your girlfriend or boyfriend? Why is college important to you?

_____

_____

_____

_____

What do you intend to achieve while in college? What are your goals?

_____

_____

_____

_____

ROADBLOCK
3

YOU can't change your PAST!

Many of my friends who dropped out of school didn't consider the consequences of their decisions. Unfortunately, today, they share how they wished they could go back in time and do things differently. But as you know, they can't go back in time. They can't change their past. They're stuck with their actions of the past.

So what happens if you don't achieve your goals while in college? What are the consequences?

_____

_____

_____

_____

_____

_____

_____

Your success or your failure is a choice. So what do you choose? Please describe the commitment that you are willing to make in order to achieve your goals.

_____

_____

_____

_____

_____

_____

_____

_____

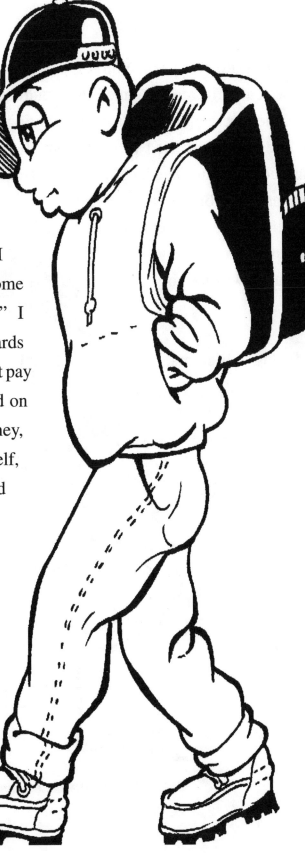

I remember one time during my second year in college. I had just finished all of my classes on Friday and was heading home. I lived in the fraternity house with sixteen other guys. While walking home, I thought about all the homework that I had due on Monday. To make matters worst, I had to take three major tests on Monday as well. I thought to myself, "Tonight, I'll eat some dinner and study five hours in my room." I had my plan. As I continued walking towards the frat house, I heard some music. I didn't pay much attention. My mind was still focused on my school work. As I continued my journey, the music got louder. I thought to myself, "Wow, someone is really partying." I started jamming to the music myself. "Bum-pop-bum-pop-pop."

As I turned the corner to walk down my street, the music got louder and louder with each step. And suddenly it hit me, the party was at my house. While walking up the driveway, I was shocked to see fraternity brothers laughing and socializing in the front yard.

One brother said, "Oh yeah, Nolram, we forgot to tell you about the party. We knew you would be ready for a good time." As I marched into the house, fraternity brothers and young ladies were eating, joking and playing various games. I walked into my room, closed the door, and tried to study, but it didn't work. I couldn't concentrate. The laughter and music were just too loud. Fraternity brothers came into my room asking me to join them. "Come on Nolram, there's plenty time to study. Put down the books and let's party."

I was facing a dilemma. What should I do — party and have fun, or do my homework and study for my three tests on Monday? I thought, "Where's the balance? How can I have the best of both worlds?"

106

What would you do if you were in my situation? Party, maybe? Be honest. Answer how you would handle this situation.

_____

_____

_____

_____

_____

_____

Well, I ended up gathering my books and walking to the library. With each step down the street, the music became softer. I thought to myself, " Man, Nolram, you're a nut— you're gonna miss all the fun." But then I realized, I can either play now and work for the rest of my life or I can work hard in college so that I will have options after college and play for the rest of my life. I resolved the conflict in my mind and felt good about my decision to study first and play later.

When I reached the library,
I was shocked!

All students have the potential to achieve and excel in school. It is just a matter of whether or not a student CHOOSES to succeed in the classroom.

Guess who was in the library?

All the students with the highest grades were there studying. It was 7:00, Friday night. Now that is some commitment, huh?

As I walked to an empty chair, I noticed my classmate James studying. I whispered to him, "I can't believe you're here on a Friday night." He looked up from his chemistry book and said, "What are you talking about Nolram? Most of us get together for a three-hour study session each night. Nolram, we get together EVERY night of the week."

At first, I was amazed by James' comments. But then I came to realize the secrets as to why some students do so well in school — they work at it. It's no mystery. Asian students are no smarter than Latino students. African-American students are no more intelligent than white students. It's very simple. Students who make a commitment to their future and study longer hours will achieve better grades.

That night, I made the commitment to study for five hours up to 12:00 midnight. Now I must be honest. It was a long time. But I had the satisfaction of completing two homework assignments. And I even studied for each of my three tests.

At 11:59, I could hardly wait for the last minute to come. BAM, midnight, I closed my books and started my journey home.

While walking through my neighborhood, I reflected upon my conversation with James. "....We get together every night to study for at least three hours in the library." As I turned the corner to walk down the street to my fraternity house, the music was jamming. There were cars lined up on both sides of the street. People were out on the lawn just "hanging." It was a "LIVE" party! As I opened the front door, I couldn't believe it — wall-to-wall people jamming to the beat. I squeezed through the people on the stairs to get to my bedroom. Once inside my bedroom, I looked at myself in the mirror and said, **"You studied hard, not it's time to party hard."**

I threw my books on the bed and ran downstairs and partied hard. I had a great time because I knew that I had taken care of business; I completed my school work.

Now it was time to celebrate. I had so much fun that I even danced on top of one of the speakers.

Realize this, either you can play now, fail some classes, and work for the rest of your life trying to get a job. Or you can work now for four years striving towards academic excellence, graduate with options, and play enjoying the rest of your life.

Now don't get me wrong. I can have just as much fun as the next student. But I wasn't going to sacrifice my goals for a few laughs. Laughs come and go. There will always be parties. But your experience in college will never repeat itself. This is an opportunity that should not be jeopardized. Life is to be enjoyed to the fullest. But take it from me, have balance: work hard and play hard.

Have you ever taken a time management class? If you haven't yet, do so immediately! Just think: each of us has the same 24 hours in a day.

So why is it that some people succeed in achieving their goals while others fail? What do you think is the reason for this?

_____

_____

_____

How a person chooses to use his or her time plays a major role in achieving success. Just think, a student has to use his or her time wisely in order to fulfill certain high school requirements in obtaining admission into college. **Take time to write the activities which you completed while in high school. For example, when did you take the PSAT and SAT examination? In what grade did you complete your college applications?**

Ninth Grade Activities: _____

Tenth Grade Activities: _____

Eleventh Grade Activities: _____

Twelfth Grade Activities: _____

How well do you manage your time? Please explain.

_____
_____
_____
_____
_____
_____
_____
_____
_____

I believe one important factor that dictates whether or not success will be achieved is determined by how well a person uses his or her time. Just think, many students are successful in obtaining admission into college. And why? It is because these students, in particular, used their time to complete certain requirements while in high school.

Successful people efficiently use their time. They stay focused on their priorities. Most of them utilize a time management system as they monitor their daily activities. Take a time management class and learn how to maximize your time by being more productive. Don't wait. Do it now!

On the next page, you see a sample time management sheet which you can photocopy. In the left hand column marked "ROLES," write (in pencil) all the various roles that you hold in your life. For me, my roles include being a son, a brother, a student, a friend, a grandson, a boyfriend, a student leader and a dreamer. Now sometimes, it can be difficult managing all these roles at once. But this time management sheet has helped many successful individuals stay on track and achieve their daily objectives. And hopefully, it will do the same for you. To obtain more information on this topic, I highly suggest you read <u>The Seven Habits of Highly Effective People</u> by Steven Covey.

My Daily Priorities

My Role	My Goals	My Priorities
Who I AM	Achievements To Reach	What To Do first

Example:

STUDENT

1. Get **A** on Math Exam.
2. Begin research on Science Term Paper.
3. Finish reading my book for report.
4. Join Science Club.
5. Go to Library -return book.

SUNDAY	MONDAY	TUESDAY	WEDNESDAY	THURSDAY	FRIDAY	SATURDAY

My Scheduled Committments

7:00	7:00	7:00	7:00	7:00	7:00	7:00
8:00	8:00	8:00	8:00	8:00	8:00	8:00
9:00	9:00	9:00	9:00	9:00	9:00	9:00
10:00	10:00	10:00	10:00	10:00	10:00	10:00
11:00	11:00	11:00	11:00	11:00	11:00	11:00
12:00	12:00	12:00	12:00	12:00	12:00	12:00
1:00	1:00	1:00	1:00	1:00	1:00	1:00
2:00	2:00	2:00	2:00	2:00	2:00	2:00
3:00	3:00	3:00	3:00	3:00	3:00	3:00
4:00	4:00	4:00	4:00	4:00	4:00	4:00
5:00	5:00	5:00	5:00	5:00	5:00	5:00
6:00	6:00	6:00	6:00	6:00	6:00	6:00
7:00	7:00	7:00	7:00	7:00	7:00	7:00
8:00	8:00	8:00	8:00	8:00	8:00	8:00

ROADBLOCK
3

After writing down all the roles that you play, list the major goals that you wish to accomplish during this upcoming week for each role.

On your time management sheet, schedule your week by writing your classes in their appropriate time slots. Next, highlight those particular time slots for which you have homework assignments, tests and quizzes. Now, on your time management sheet, schedule time to study and complete your homework for each day.

After writing out your school schedule, including classes and study time, you will now schedule time to complete your most-important, weekly goals. Review your weekly goals and prioritize the most important goals with the following ranking:

A - "Very important. Must be done this week."
B - "Somewhat important, but not critical."
C - "Not really important. Can wait until next week if need be."

Give a priority to each goal. Prioritize all "A" goals by writing down "A1," "A2," "A3,"..... with "1" signifying the most important "A" goal. Next, prioritize the "B" and "C" goals. Schedule time slots for all goals receiving an "A" ranking on your sheet (beginning with "A1" first, followed by "A2" and so on until all "A" goals have been scheduled). During this time period, you will only be focused on completing your "A" goals. If time is still available, schedule time slots for your goals receiving a "B" ranking. Next, schedule time slots to complete your goals receiving a "C" ranking.

Feels good, huh? You've got your week planned. Everything is fine, right? Well, not exactly! Believe me, life never goes the way you plan. No matter how well you plan, things will always come up. For instance, you think an activity is only going to take an hour to complete. But rather, it ends up taking five hours. Don't get mad, just be flexible. And make sure your pencil has an eraser.

By taking time to schedule your upcoming week, you will be proactive in making things happen in your life. Rather than reacting to everything else and losing your focus, you will now be empowered and in control because of your time management system.

Believe me, you can have the best intentions of studying and completing your school work. But because you didn't have a time management system, you can get caught up in just having a good time and lose focus.

Let me ask you a serious question: Are a few laughs worth possibly jeopardizing your goals? Answer why or why not. Be honest.

_____

_____

_____

_____

_____

_____

Just like all of my friends, you probably answered "NO." Even those friends who failed out of school answered "NO" as well.

So what's the difference? What allows one college student to succeed and graduate while another fails? What do you think is the reason for this? Please explain.

_____

_____

_____

_____

_____

_____

_____

_____

_____

_____

_____

In certain situations, I believe that some students can not handle the personal freedom. In college, you have a tremendous amount of freedom. On the campus, there's no mom or dad waking you up for your first morning class.

Have you ever overslept and were late for school? Through elementary school to high school, there were many teachers who would call your parents if you were acting up or not performing up to your true potential in class. Remember those teacher-parent conversations on the phone?

However, in college, it is highly unlikely that a professor will call your parents if you miss class. There is no telephone call home if you do not turn in an assignment or happen to fail a test. In some classes, you could just be a social security number to the professor. I have taken some classes in a big lecture hall with as many as 400 other students. The professor had no way of knowing if I was there or not.

So basically, you are responsible for your success in college. What will you do to handle this freedom and ensure your success? What will you specifically do to reach your goals?

_____

_____

_____

_____

_____

Some friends failed in achieving their goals while in college because they lost their focus. Instead of studying for that upcoming final examination, they would succumb to peer pressure and party all night long. Unfortunately, no one was partying when they received their corrected examination marked with an "F."

So how do you stay focused? I already shared with you the importance of creating a **Dream/Collage** (refer to page 54 for more details). This collage will help you maintain your focus as to what's really important.

Another suggestion is to **write your goals on index cards.** Carry these index cards with you everywhere you go. Review these index cards every chance you get throughout the day. Pull out your index cards as you walk to class, to the cafeteria, and even to the bathroom.

One key to success is keeping your goals in front of you. Put your goals everywhere: on your bathroom mirror, on your refrigerator, on your bathroom door, on your car dashboard.

Your goals will become real and your life will take on new meaning. You'll be empowered.

Now that you have your goals and a serious focus, the next step is developing a game plan.

Let me ask you a serious question. Do you plan to fail? Please explain your answer.

_____

_____

_____

Probably not, but the real question is, "Are you failing to plan?" Be honest.

_____

_____

_____

_____

Everyone has dreams. Everyone has goals. However, many people never reach their goals or manifest their dreams. **Successful individuals develop a plan and then take action using their time management system.** For example, what type of grades do you want to obtain on your next report card? List each of your classes and write the desired grade which you are striving to obtain for that particular class.

_____

_____

What is your plan to achieve these grades?

_____

_____

More Study Tips

Now that you have determined your desired grades, it's time to get busy. In addition to the advice offered in "Success Keys for Succeeding In School" (found on page 93), here are three more ways to achieve your desired grades.

1. **Talk** to each professor and share the desired grade that you are seeking to obtain in that particular class. Be up front and direct with your professors. Ask each professor to explain what specifically will be required to achieve your desired grade. Do not leave the professor's office until you clearly understand the grading system for the class. Put all tests, quizzes, homework assignments and other due dates on your calendar. Remember, there is power in managing your time.

2. **Commit** to spending a specific number of hours in the library each and every day. After my conversation with James, I realized that "smart" students do well in school, not because they're so "smart," but rather, it's because they study everyday. It's that plain and simple. Because of this, I made the commitment to spend at least four hours each and every day in the library. From 3:00 PM to 7:00 PM, seven days a week, I was in the library. It became a habit. This commitment empowered my life. This made the difference between failing a class and receiving an "A+." How many hours in the library will you commit to studying every day? _____ Make the commitment. No matter what, make the commitment to be in the library studying for that number of hours, each and every day.

Many students procrastinate until the night before their class assignment is due. It comes down to them staying up and cramming the entire course material all night long. Why experience all this pressure and stress if it can be avoided? It doesn't have to be that way. By making your study session a daily habit, you will understand each class lesson and not fall behind. And as a result of keeping up with each lesson, you will achieve your academic goals.

3. **Read** the upcoming chapter of your text book before your teacher reviews it in class. This will give you an opportunity to better understand the upcoming lesson because it will not be something new to you when the teacher lectures in class.

What To Do Outside
The Classroom

Enough of the academic suggestions. As we both know, you're in school to get an education. I'm sure you'll take care of business, right? Let's move on and discuss another type of education— the education which takes place outside the classroom.

Although there is critical information being presented within the classroom, many leadership skills are developed outside the classroom.

In school, with what extracurricular organizations are you currently involved? Which organizations are you considering joining?

_____

_____

_____

_____

_____

What have you learned from your involvement in these organizations? Be specific.

_____

_____

_____

_____

_____

_____

Take on leadership roles. Become an officer of your organization as soon as possible. I did not realize the importance of being a school leader until I was a junior in college. During my freshman and sophomore year, I just followed the group. But in the fall semester of my junior year, my fraternity brothers elected me to become chairperson of the service committee. I was nervous at first because I had never done anything like this before.

I was scared. Would I fail?...

Be A Leader

My fear was natural because I had never experienced anything like this before. But I'm glad that I faced my fears because it turned out to be a great experience. After applying myself in this new role, I became excited about the idea of developing my leadership skills. Because of this experience, I became more confident in my abilities. I wish that I had taken on leadership positions while I was in middle school and high school. Please learn from my experience and don't wait. **Get involved today.** Join an organization at your school and become a student leader. Give yourself a gift by experiencing various positions of leadership. It will change your life. And believe me, if I could successfully do it, so can you. I went from being a shy, insecure follower to becoming a sincere and positive leader. Because of my leadership involvement in various organizations, my life has changed for the better!

By being a student leader, you will acquire a critical education that can not be necessarily taught within the classroom. You learn how to motivate your peers. You learn how to organize your thoughts as well as how to run a meeting. You learn people skills. And in addition to these benefits, there are many more skills that you will acquire.

This leadership role will improve the quality of your life.

Another reason to obtain positions of leadership is because colleges and corporations look favorably upon students who were officers within their respective organizations.

Get
Corporate Experience
During Your
Collegiate Career

Since I've mentioned the corporation, let's take a further look at employment opportunities during your collegiate career.

What type of company do you plan to work for after college?

_____

_____

Why wait? During the summer vacation of your collegiate career, work for that dream corporation. And by the way, do not overlook taking advantage of winter and spring break. Investigate working in an internship for one week during these school breaks as well.

Some of you may be saying, "Nolram, I agreed with you so far. But now you're stretching. This is crazy. You want me to work during my vacation."

YES, THAT'S ABSOLUTELY RIGHT!
GET CORPORATE EXPERIENCE
DURING YOUR COLLEGIATE CAREER!

**How would you feel if you had a 4.0 GPA (all "A's")
only to be rejected
and not given a job offer
from your dream corporation?**

.......What would you do next?

It may sound crazy, but I've seen it happen. Many corporations are not only looking for college graduates who have excellent grades. In addition to the grades, corporations are seeking students who are well-rounded and have work experience in the field of their studies. Being affiliated in various extracurricular activities and organizations exposes you to new opportunities, people, situations and experiences. By expanding your experiences, you grow.

And Corporations value this experience.

Let's be serious. It's competitive out here. Recruiters are seeking the best candidates for their corporations. Think for a few minutes and write down some of your personal assets and strengths that make you stand out.

_____

_____

_____

_____

_____

Why should a company choose you among the other hundred college students applying for the same job? When a company asks you to write the reasons why they should hire you, what are you going to write?

_____

_____

_____

_____

Get a head start and work for that dream company either during your summer, spring or winter break. It offers many benefits which can make a difference. It gives the corporation an opportunity to see you in action. Relationships will be developed. You will gain exposure to Corporate America. You will apply class theories to real-life situations during your corporate internship. And you will return to school more enlightened.

Now is the time for YOU to gain that exposure by obtaining that CORPORATE EXPERIENCE!

From your corporate experience, you will definitely obtain a glimpse of what your future job after college will entail. And who knows, after working this summer, you may discover that you do not like that particular "dream" job. Wouldn't it be a shame if you studied long hours for four or five years in college to graduate and work in a job that you hate? This happens all the time. Sadly enough, I have some friends who hate their present jobs. And others even dislike their companies. Just think, this could have all been avoided.

With an internship during your collegiate career, you will gain a glimpse of what your future corporate position may entail.

I want to know whether or not I will like a particular job. At least during a 3-month summer internship, I can gain some insight. Otherwise, after graduating from college, I could feel trapped in a full-time, long-term commitment that I dislike because the job is not what I had expected.

What about you? When do you want to discover if a particular job is for you? Now or later?

Now is the time for you to gain that exposure by obtaining that corporate experience today.

In College,
you are totally responsible for your outcome.
You and only you!

Be honest, give yourself an "A", "C", or "F" in your commitment to your studies. Answer here. _____
If it's not an "A", what will you do to improve your grade in this particular area?

_____

_____

_____

_____

Be honest, give yourself an "A", "C", or "F" in your involvement in extracurricular activities. Answer here. _____
If it's not an "A", what will you do to improve your grade in this particular area?

_____

_____

_____

_____

Be honest, give yourself an "A", "C", or "F" in holding positions of leadership in your school. Answer here. _____
If it's not an "A", what will you do to improve your grade in this particular area?

_____

_____

_____

_____

Be honest, give yourself an "A", "C", or "F" in obtaining work experience while you are a student. Answer here. _____
If it's not an "A", what will you do to improve your grade in this particular area?

_____

_____

_____

_____

YES!

Four grades! Did you obtain straight "A's"? If not, I'm sure you'll implement these success keys and have an outstanding college experience. Let me ask you a question, "Do you want to succeed in college as well as on your job?" _____ YES _____NO

You probably answered, "Yes." And that is why you must plan your success. You do not plan to fail so let's not fail to plan.

Remember the 7P's: *"Prior Proper Planning Prevents Pathetically Poor Performance."*

In your plan to achieve success, be sure to seek computer expertise. No matter what your future goals or dreams are, plan on becoming knowledgeable of computers because computers are the wave of the future. Your knowledge of computers will definitely impact your future.

Congratulations,

you have now gained an understanding of how to surpass the potential roadblock known as "Failing in College."

You are making things happen!

You're on the journey to unlimited success.

OPPORTUNITY

Congratulations!

YOU DID IT !

◆

YOU NOW POSSESS THE TEN SUCCESS KEYS

Congratulations!
You did it.
You have read this entire book.

You now possess the TEN Success Keys:

1. Understanding the power of choices in this maze called "LIFE"
2. Growing through challenges by learning lessons
3. Realizing you're worth a billion dollars
4. Developing a plan for your personal growth
5. Writing in your success journal
6. Becoming clear on your goals
7. Succeeding in school by utilizing the tips for academic excellence
8. Standing up for your dreams and not succumbing to negative peer pressure
9. Excelling outside the classroom through positions of leadership
10. Planning your success by managing your time

You should be proud of yourself. You are a leader who has chosen success. By answering all the questions and incorporating the various exercises in your daily life, you will manifest your true potential. Your dreams will soon become a reality.

You have learned strategies for dealing with various life challenges. By reading my story, you have been enlightened as to how my choices and decisions impacted my life. Hopefully, you have learned from my mistakes, and will not encounter the same negative consequences. Congratulations! You have chosen your success. Smile, you are on the journey to success!

TAKING RESPONSIBILITY

Thank you for reading this book. Share it with a friend if it has helped you. As you already know, the younger me was good at blaming others. At times, my life was really upside-down. I was so confused about where I was heading.

You know my story well. You see, this book has been about many people, including you. In fact, what is MARLON spelled backwards?

That is correct, NOLRAM! Surprise, Surprise! NOLRAM was just the confused Marlon of the past. Nolram is in all of us because we all make mistakes. That's just life.

No matter what you do, you're going to make mistakes. But don't beat yourself up because of something you did in the past. Just learn the lessons and continue your journey through the maze called "Life." The beauty of life is that no matter what has happened in the past, today is a new day. All you have to do is THINK first before taking action. Remember, the decisions and choices you make today will greatly impact your future.

Fortunately, a blessed MARLON broke through this destructive NOLRAM shell and is now moving forward in a positive direction!

And the same thing will happen for you. If I can do it so can you! Learn from your past and grow.

However, there will be times when you feel like you're not moving forward in life. There may even be situations when you are totally confused about we to do next. Sometimes, you may not be sure as to which door to choose. And unfortunately, your choices may lead to nega-tive consequences. But remember, as long as you learn a lesson, you have grown.

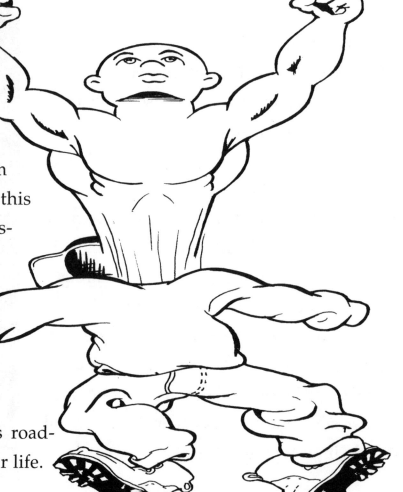

As I broke out of the Nolram shell, so did you. By reading this book and answering the ques-tions and completing the various exercises, you've grown and become a better person. You are now empowered to more effectively handle the various road-blocks that may pop up in your life.

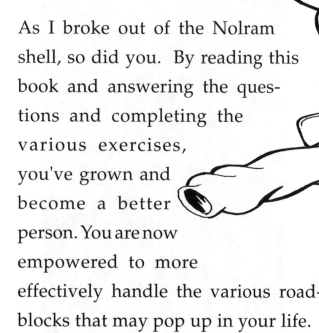

As of now, you are claiming your success. In each chapter, I've shared various issues with you. In fact, at this very moment, you may be facing some of these exact situations.

I'm not saying that I have all the answers but I wrote this book to share some thoughts to help empower you. Right now, you may be looking at your future with a BIG question mark. Hopefully, this book has motivated you and empowered you with some success strategies for taking responsibility for your future.

The name of my company is Success By Choice. The reason for starting a company with this name is because one day I had a major transformation. I finally stopped blaming others for my present state and condition. These were just excuses. The reason that I'm the way that I am is not because of my parents or employer or teachers or even society as a whole.

In my younger days, I blamed everyone else for my present situation. It was an easy way out. I did not have to assume responsibility for my future or even my life. Fortunately, I finally realized how silly this was. Think about it. By blaming or criticizing someone else, does that empower you? Does that make YOU a better person? By blaming others, are you growing? Take responsibility and shout out loud, "My success is my choice." Why? Because, it is.......... YOUR CHOICE!

Hoorah, YOU'RE DOING IT!!! You're On The Road To Happiness

Once I realized that my life is my responsibility, my future took on a new meaning. And the same thing will happen for you. Consider it as though you are a movie director and you are writing out the next scenes to your movie. And guess what, you are the main star as well. Yes, that's right. YOU are the main star as well as the movie producer. So tell me, how is your movie going to turn out? Will it be a sad, tear-jerking movie or will it be a comedy? Will it be an adventure? Or maybe, it will be a combination of many things. You tell me, because it's in your hands. The purpose of this book is to get you fired up on making your top blockbuster movie. Always remember and never forget this quote: "My success is my choice." In fact, memorize it.

So let's get it on.
Take one, here we go.
Five, four, three, two,
one,.............
sound,.........
lighting,...........
ACTION.

Your best-seller movie
is entitled

*"My Success
is My Choice."*

Please feel free to complete

the following questionnaire

and mail it to

Success By Choice.

I pray this book has helped you.

By learning

from my various challenges,

you will hopefully

not make the same mistakes.

Remember, enjoy life to the fullest.

Complete the EVALUATION on the reverse side!

PLEASE MAIL THIS FORM TO :

Success By Choice
Attention:
"What's Up?"
25125 Santa Clara St.
321
Hayward, CA 94544

"What's Up?"
Evaluation Questionnaire

Your responses will be helpful in improving our series of books.

Thank you for your participation.

Circle the number in each box which reflects your opinion.

1. **Were any of Nolram's experiences similar to your own?** (NOT AT ALL) | 1 | 2 | 3 | 4 | (DEFINITELY)

2. **Did Nolram's experiences help you better understand the importance of <u>your</u> choices in <u>your</u> future?** (NOT AT ALL) | 1 | 2 | 3 | 4 | (DEFINITELY)

3. **Did you enjoy reading this book? Was it fun?** (NOT AT ALL) | 1 | 2 | 3 | 4 | (DEFINITELY)

4. **Did you complete ALL of the suggested exercises?** (NOT AT ALL) | 1 | 2 | 3 | 4 | (DEFINITELY)

5. **Did you enjoy creating your Dreams/Collage?** (NOT AT ALL) | 1 | 2 | 3 | 4 | (DEFINITELY)

6. **Will you use what you learned from Nolram in your own life experiences?** (NOT AT ALL) | 1 | 2 | 3 | 4 | (DEFINITELY)

7. **Do you want to read more books like "What's Up?"** (NOT AT ALL) | 1 | 2 | 3 | 4 | (DEFINITELY)

What were your favorite sections of this book?

_____

_____

What suggestions do you have for improving this book?

_____

_____

Additional Comments?

_____

_____

Success By Choice Order Form

"What's Up?" is helping our young people discover their **True Greatness!** Join in their excitement!... and celebrate, today! **Order Now!**

ITEM DESCRIPTION	QTY	UNIT PRICE	TOTAL
A. BOOK: "What's Up?"		$15	
B. AUDIO TAPE: "Living Your Dreams Now"		$12	
C. SPECIAL BONUS/ BOOK & TAPE — "What's Up?" & "Living Your Dreams Now"		$20	

☐ Check ☐ Money Order ☐ VISA ☐ AMEX ☐ MASTERCARD

CREDIT CARD NO.

EXPIRATION DATE

AUTHORIZED SIGNATURE

DRIVER'S LICENSE NO.

Make Checks Payable To & Mail Order Form To:
Success By Choice
25125 Santa Clara Street
Suite #321
Hayward, CA 94544
(510) 887-1311

Sub-Total	
Sales Tax (CA add 8.25%)	
Shipping/ Handling	$5.00
Total	$

Want to be on our Mailing List?
Please complete the information:

NAME   PHONE

ADDRESS   CITY   STATE   ZIP

✂ -

Success By Choice Order Form

"What's Up?" is helping our young people discover their **True Greatness!** Join in their excitement!... and celebrate, today! **Order Now!**

ITEM DESCRIPTION	QTY	UNIT PRICE	TOTAL
A. BOOK: "What's Up?"		$15	
B. AUDIO TAPE: "Living Your Dreams Now"		$12	
C. SPECIAL BONUS/ BOOK & TAPE — "What's Up?" & "Living Your Dreams Now"		$20	

☐ Check ☐ Money Order ☐ VISA ☐ AMEX ☐ MASTERCARD

CREDIT CARD NO.

EXPIRATION DATE

AUTHORIZED SIGNATURE

DRIVER'S LICENSE NO.

Make Checks Payable To & Mail Order Form To:
Success By Choice
25125 Santa Clara Street
Suite #321
Hayward, CA 94544
(510) 887-1311

Sub-Total	
Sales Tax (CA add 8.25%)	
Shipping/ Handling	$5.00
Total	$

Want to be on our Mailing List?
Please complete the information:

NAME   PHONE

ADDRESS   CITY   STATE   ZIP

✂ -

Success By Choice Order Form

"What's Up?" is helping our young people discover their **True Greatness!** Join in their excitement!... and celebrate, today! **Order Now!**

ITEM DESCRIPTION	QTY	UNIT PRICE	TOTAL
A. BOOK: "What's Up?"		$15	
B. AUDIO TAPE: "Living Your Dreams Now"		$12	
C. SPECIAL BONUS/ BOOK & TAPE — "What's Up?" & "Living Your Dreams Now"		$20	

☐ Check ☐ Money Order ☐ VISA ☐ AMEX ☐ MASTERCARD

CREDIT CARD NO.

EXPIRATION DATE

AUTHORIZED SIGNATURE

DRIVER'S LICENSE NO.

Make Checks Payable To & Mail Order Form To:
Success By Choice
25125 Santa Clara Street
Suite #321
Hayward, CA 94544
(510) 887-1311

Sub-Total	
Sales Tax (CA add 8.25%)	
Shipping/ Handling	$5.00
Total	$

Want to be on our Mailing List?
Please complete the information:

NAME   PHONE

ADDRESS   CITY   STATE   ZIP

Success By Choice Order Form

ITEM DESCRIPTION	QTY	UNIT PRICE	SUB-TOTAL
★ What's Up? (BEST SELLER)		x $15.00	=
THE HELP ME! WORKBOOK SERIES:			
1. Playing Around (Random Sex)		x $ 7.00	=
2. Falling To Drugs And Alcohol Addiction		x $ 7.00	=
3. Succumbing To Negative Peer Pressure		x $ 7.00	=
4. Battling With Parents (It's Me Against Them)		x $ 7.00	=
5. Being Prejudiced And Hating Others		x $ 7.00	=
6. Moaning And Not Working		x $ 7.00	=
7. Crying With No Money		x $ 7.00	=
8. Fearing Leadership		x $ 7.00	=
9. Lacking A Spiritual Relationship		x $ 7.00	=
WORKBOOK SUB-TOTAL			=
MOTIVATIONAL TAPES:			
1. "Living Your Dreams Now" Audio Tape		x $12.00	=
2. "GAPAPS" (Goals, Attitude, Plan, Action, Persistence, Success)		x $12.00	=
3. Instructional Video Tape & Lesson Plans		x $250.00	=
MOTIVATIONAL TAPE SUB-TOTAL			=

**Mail Order Form &
Make Checks Payable To:**

Success By Choice
25125 Santa Clara Street
Suite #321
Hayward, CA 94544
(510) 887-1311

SUB-TOTAL	=
SALES TAX (CA ADD 8.25%)	=
SHIPPING & HANDLING	= $5.00
TOTAL AMOUNT DUE	=

We Accept:
❑ Check   ❑ Master Card
❑ Money Order ❑ American Express
❑ Visa

CREDIT NO.	NAME
EXPIRATION DATE	ADDRESS
AUTHORIZED SIGNATURE	CITY, STATE, ZIP
DRIVER'S LICENSE NO.	DAY PHONE EVENING PHONE

Success By Choice Order Form

ITEM DESCRIPTION	QTY	UNIT PRICE	SUB-TOTAL
★ What's Up? (BEST SELLER)		x $15.00	=
THE HELP ME! WORKBOOK SERIES:			
1. Playing Around (Random Sex)		x $ 7.00	=
2. Falling To Drugs And Alcohol Addiction		x $ 7.00	=
3. Succumbing To Negative Peer Pressure		x $ 7.00	=
4. Battling With Parents (It's Me Against Them)		x $ 7.00	=
5. Being Prejudiced And Hating Others		x $ 7.00	=
6. Moaning And Not Working		x $ 7.00	=
7. Crying With No Money		x $ 7.00	=
8. Fearing Leadership		x $ 7.00	=
9. Lacking A Spiritual Relationship		x $ 7.00	=
WORKBOOK SUB-TOTAL			=
MOTIVATIONAL TAPES:			
1. "Living Your Dreams Now" Audio Tape		x $12.00	=
2. "GAPAPS" (Goals, Attitude, Plan, Action, Persistence, Success)		x $12.00	=
3. Instructional Video Tape & Lesson Plans		x $250.00	=
MOTIVATIONAL TAPE SUB-TOTAL			=

**Mail Order Form &
Make Checks Payable To:**

Success By Choice
25125 Santa Clara Street
Suite #321
Hayward, CA 94544
(510) 887-1311

SUB-TOTAL	=
SALES TAX (CA ADD 8.25%)	=
SHIPPING & HANDLING	= $5.00
TOTAL AMOUNT DUE	=

We Accept:
- ❏ Check
- ❏ Money Order
- ❏ Visa
- ❏ Master Card
- ❏ American Express

CREDIT NO. _____

EXPIRATION DATE _____

AUTHORIZED SIGNATURE _____

DRIVER'S LICENSE NO. _____

NAME _____

ADDRESS _____

CITY, STATE, ZIP _____

DAY PHONE _____ EVENING PHONE _____